PRESENTED TO:

_____

PRESENTED BY:

_____

DATE:

_____

Children are not casual guests in our home.
They have been loaned to us temporarily
for the purpose of loving them
and instilling a foundation of values on which
their future lives will be built.

James Dobson

101 THINGS YOU SHOULD DO BEFORE YOUR KIDS LEAVE HOME

DAVID BORDON AND TOM WINTERS

Faith
Words

New York Boston Nashville

101 Things You Should Do Before Your Kids Leave Home
Copyright © 2007 Bordon-Winters LLC

Project developed by Bordon Books, Tulsa, Oklahoma
Concept: David Bordon and Tom Winters
Project Writing: John T. Perrodin, Colorado Springs, CO, in association with SnapdragonGroup[SM] Editorial Services

Unless otherwise indicated, Scripture quotations are taken from the *Holy Bible: New International Version*®. NIV®.(North American Edition)®. Copyright © 1973, 1978, 1984 by International Bible Society. Used by permission of Zondervan Publishing House. All rights reserved.

Scripture quotations marked KJV are taken from the *King James Version* of the Bible.

Scripture quotations marked MSG are taken from *The Message* © 1993. Used by permission of NavPress Publishing Group.

FaithWords
Hachette BookGroup USA
1271 Avenue of the Americas, New York, NY 10020
Visit our Web site at www.faithwords.com

The FaithWords name and logo are trademarks of Hachette Book Group USA.

Printed in Singapore
First Edition: April 2007
10 9 8 7 6 5 4 3 2 1

ISBN: 0-446-57919-X
ISBN-13: 978-0-446-57919-3

INTRODUCTION

Eighteen years, maybe twenty: that's about all the time you will have to prepare your kids to be happy, responsible, independent, peace-loving citizens of the world into which they were born. That might seem like a reasonably long time on the day you bring that little bundle of joy home from the hospital—but in the scheme of things, it's really just a blink. One blink—that's all the time you have to go after moments of joy, moments of love, moments of learning with a deep resolve to get and give all you can, while you can.

The book you hold in your hands, *101 Things You Should Do Before Your Kids Leave Home,* was written to help you map out those precious years. It's filled with ideas and advice designed to help you maximize your ability to send your children out into the world with all the tools they need to succeed, while making sure you and your kids enjoy every precious moment. So go ahead and read, learn, laugh, sing, swim, and fly a kite. Your children are God's gracious gift—a gift so great, you'll need His help to comprehend it.

CONTENTS

101 THINGS YOU SHOULD DO BEFORE YOUR KIDS LEAVE HOME

1

PLANT A
FAMILY
TREE

Our kids grow up so fast. In a mere cosmic blink, they're adults ready to launch out into the world on their own. A wise parent must search out opportunities to instill a sense of family—a tight circle in a wide world, a bond they can always depend on.

That can be as simple and beautiful as planting a family tree.

Involve the whole family in the task of choosing a location for your tree. That might be your own yard, a park, or even a public roadway. Make sure you select a place where you and your family will always be able to visit your tree.

Once you've found an ideal place, ask a professional to advise you concerning the type of tree that is best suited for your area and climate. Make sure the chosen location has the right amount of sunlight and room to grow. Then pile everyone into the car and go together to bring your family tree home.

Encourage each person to take a turn with the shovel and throw in a handful of dirt when the tree is in place. When you've tamped it down, take hands around the tree and offer a prayer of thanksgiving to God for your family—who you are and what you will become. If possible, take pictures of your family around the tree each year. It's fun to compare later pictures with those of your kids encircling a wobbly little stick.

God so values the concept of family that He instituted it way back in the Garden of Eden. In spiritual terms, He calls us His children, part of His own eternal family. Before your kids sprout wings and fly away from you, give them a symbol of your family's strength and commitment.

2

OPEN A SNOW-CONE STAND

W hat's better than ice water on a blistering summer day? Shaved ice soaked in thick, fruity syrup. Yum! The classic snow cone is a hot neighborhood seller on warm afternoons. Let your kids set up shop. Maybe they'll even make some spare change. Before breaking into business with your children, remember the snow-cone motto: flavor matters.

That means your kids have some big decisions. Will they opt for grape, cherry, lime, strawberry, orange, or raspberry? With a little Web hopping, you can come up with strawberry kiwi, root beer, and winter watermelon. Check out The Canning Pantry at *www.canning-pantry.com* and look over their luscious shaved ice flavors.

You can purchase a stand or build one yourself if you're so inclined. Even if it's a simple tarp, the stand should have a roof to prevent overexposure to the sun. And make sure you're always supervising for safety's sake.

Going into the snow-cone business will teach your children a powerful truth. God gives everyone different likes and dislikes, interests, and abilities. One child may be all about scooping, another completely absorbed with pouring on the flavors. Another may be gifted at marketing and slogans. If so, let your artist make signs that are colorful and easy to read. If one's skill is sales, put the convincing spokesperson up front to pull in the crowds. Should one shine at customer service, have him or her serve up neat snow cones with a big paper napkin.

Every child can pitch in. No shirkers and no exceptions. Working together to open up a sidewalk snow-cone stand provides a great lesson in business management and serving others—skills your children will appreciate long after they leave home.

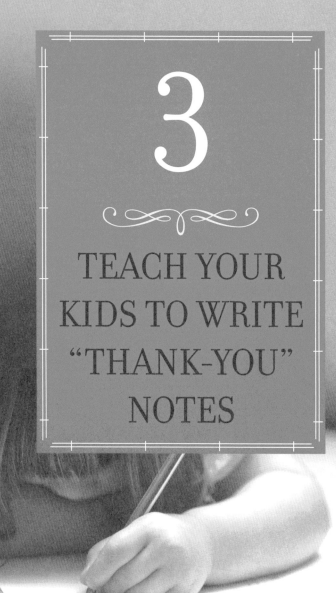

3

TEACH YOUR KIDS TO WRITE "THANK-YOU" NOTES

Once upon a time parents promoted an unwritten rule: You can't play with a new toy until you write a "thank-you" note. That may seem archaic to those unfamiliar with such civility, but it was a great way to get children to pause for a moment of gratitude before enjoying the rewards of a loved one's benevolence.

Thank-you notes don't have to be long, complicated affairs. A child need only mention the fun and/or informative elements of the item and how grateful he or she is for the gift-giver's kindness. If a child is too young to write, you can be their scribe—and encourager. Put some kisses and hugs at the end for the younger kids or let them add some of their art work. Older kids should be encouraged to add a few loving words, and that's really all there is to it. Simple, but effective. The effort's as good for the child as the person getting the note.

The Bible tells a story of ten lepers who were all healed by Jesus. Nine ran on to family and friends, delighted at their good fortune. Only one stopped to say "thanks." It's an important lesson. We constantly enjoy God's gracious gifts and frequently forget to offer thanks. Still He continually showers blessings upon even those who don't recognize His goodness.

In truth, it takes such a small effort to show appreciation. When children write a note of thanks, they pull back on the urge to expect the world or the World Maker to cater to their personal wish list. Inborn greed gets a kick in the seat when kids learn to give thanks where and when it is due.

4

SAIL OVER YOUR HOUSE IN A HOT-AIR BALLOON

I magine sailing high above the trees and rooftops—you and your kids, as free as birds on the wing. It's an unforgettable experience that will trigger fanciful memories for a lifetime.

This favorite of fun lovers around the globe has another important benefit: it provides a unique perspective on life. As you float high above, earthbound images blur, imperfections vanish, little troubles fade. From your lofty perch, you see only ordered streets, neatly appointed lawns, and beautiful blue bodies of water. You could even say that it's a God's-eye view!

Hot-air balloon rides were once a delight enjoyed only by the most daring, but now they are far more accessible. You can soar into the clear, blue sky at county fairs, fund-raising events, and balloon festivals. In many places, it's as simple as checking your local yellow pages or the Internet. You can learn where to get a balloon ride, how balloons fly, or how to become a balloon pilot. You should also know that such life-lifting adventures are often available to anyone willing to volunteer as part of the ground crew. Ask the balloon owner if you and your kids can have a trip to the clouds as payment for your labors.

A family hot-air balloon ride may seem like an extravagance when you're working hard to put food on the table, but it's one that may be worth digging down deep for. Before they leave home, your kids will have a priceless illustration of how God can lift us high above our problems and carry us on angels' wings through the toughest moments of our lives.

5

❦

SHARE
FAMILY
RECIPES

Comfort food: for some that's a large part of being a family. It means sitting down to Grandma's famous meatloaf or enjoying Dad's eye-watering spicy sausage stuffing. That's how we learn to enjoy family favorites—one taste at a time. But those traditions will slip away unless you open up the recipe box and teach your children the secrets of making your mealtime masterpieces.

Many kids, raised on fast food or other meals out, don't have the chance to enjoy the pleasures of home cooking. Even if you or your forebears are culinarily challenged, you can still show your children how to make some good old-fashioned recipes.

With prechopped veggies, precooked meats, and prepared sauces, it's easy to take a few shortcuts and still serve a scrumptious success. To start, show your children how to use a recipe book or surf for a particular dish online. Turn on the oven; gather what's needed from the pantry, fridge, or freezer; measure out portions; and mix up a classic. You can do it!

Not everyone is a gifted cook, but anyone can follow a recipe, especially a tried-and-true favorite. (Ask your mom for easy ones if you're timid.) Cooking teaches kids that ingredients need to be added and mixed in a specific order. Bread won't rise without yeast; spaghetti sauce won't taste the same if you make it with refried beans. You get the idea.

Use that as a way to talk to your children about how God wants us to follow a set recipe in our relationship with Him. Prayer, trust, and a huge helping of faith—all must be combined to make our friendship with Him grow. And as parents we have the inestimable privilege of imparting this recipe for life to our children.

6

CHECK OUT LIFE—AND FAITH—IN OTHER LANDS

L earning about foreign lands and peoples can broaden your appreciation for your own culture. Better still, it teaches your kids to resist the urge to instantly brand something different as wrong. However, understanding distinctions is crucial to building discernment.

Begin the exploration by hopping online to find where your children will find out about various cultures in a kid-friendly format. You'll be intrigued at the wealth of information available. With a few more searches or mouse clicks, you'll find photos, recipes, and stories about the land you're exploring together.

Children need to realize that not all governments rule fairly, however, and sometimes differences count to the core—especially when the topic is God. Your children should know that there are people who sacrifice freedom, and perhaps their lives, to worship as they believe.

Help your kids ask the right questions. Does the religion of a certain country support the freedom to worship as a person sees fit? Christianity allows people to choose for themselves whether or not to believe in God, let alone serve Him. Many other religions won't tolerate such openness and consider outsiders heretics. Teach your children to cherish their freedoms and pray for those who do not have the same privileges.

Your children will find much good in other cultures and see that certain differences don't matter. They can and should learn to enjoy other ways of communicating, eating, playing, dancing, and dressing. But when it comes to personal faith, not all cultures are the same. Pretending otherwise undermines our beliefs, confuses our children, and does great disservice to the God we trust.

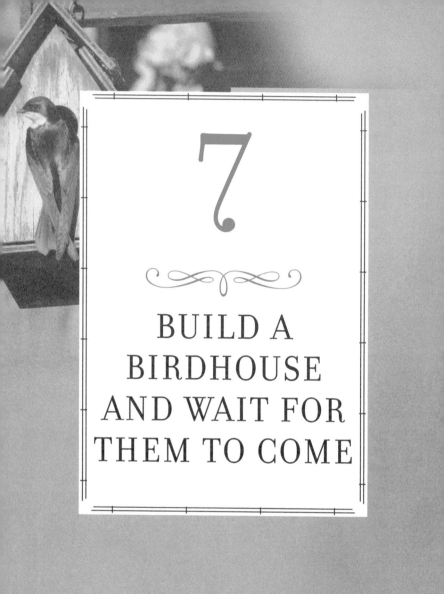

7

BUILD A
BIRDHOUSE
AND WAIT FOR
THEM TO COME

Birds are wonderfully diverse. Some sing, some delight the eye, and some fuss and fume at their feathered foes. All are fascinating and worth the time it takes to get to know them. With a little togetherness, you and your kids can discover a new adventure: backyard birding!

First things first. Start by building a birdhouse from bits of unneeded wood, some glue, and a few old nails from the workbench. You may want to go online to get simple instructions for creating a refuge for a few of God's flightiest creatures. Some patterns use only three pieces of wood and even the least handy should succeed at the construction. The library is also full of woodworking books that will give you ideas for building more intricate abodes.

Check out resources that will allow you and your children to identify the birds you can expect in your locale. You can also find out what seeds to provide to keep their younglings well fed. If your crew is enthusiastic, you could even provide nesting materials for your new bird friends—a much better alternative than watching them defluff your patio cushions.

Encourage your youngsters to record the variety of feathered visits, dating each new sighting and even snapping pictures of unusual visitors. This will keep the kids' interest and excitement alive for years to come.

God calls us to care for His creation. Helping your children build a cozy birds' home gives them a taste of what stewardship of the planet means. As you provide a place for the birds to escape the storms of life, your kids will also gain a glimpse of God's constant care for them.

8

MAKE YOUR KIDS HOME-MOVIE STARS

Making your children movie stars has never been easier. With the glut of digital video cameras and home-editing equipment available, you can create productions of a quality undreamed of by our parents and grandparents. You and your children can easily capture once-in-a-lifetime events and create a priceless family history.

Before you begin, be sure to go online or to the library to get ideas and tips. You and your kids will be glad you did your homework when you see the final results.

One surefire hint for better video: be sure you have a baby or child on-screen. You can't go wrong if you feature lots of life, activity, and movement. When it comes to cataloging your family on video, try to include birthdays, holidays, special vacations, and other highlights. Don't attempt to film everything, but it's definitely okay to shoot more than you need if you plan to edit later.

As your children grow older, turn over the camera to them on occasion, freeing yourself to be on-screen for a change. You may end up with an avant-garde approach, but go with it. Let them expand their creativity.

The home movies your children shoot will become family heirlooms for a new generation, a visual scrapbook of moments of joy that have passed into eternity. One day you'll weep and smile to see missing loved ones live on TV.

God doesn't promise us a set number of smiles, a certain number of hugs. You have no guarantees, no idea how long you'll have with your children. That's why the fun filmed today will turn to treasure tomorrow.

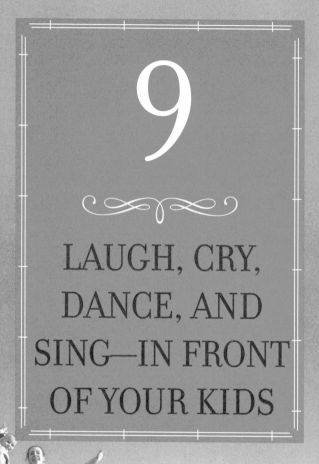

9

LAUGH, CRY,
DANCE, AND
SING—IN FRONT
OF YOUR KIDS

The laughing and dancing part comes easy. Often they go together. Your child's giggles follow your jiggles. Your children know better than anyone how parents can be struck goofy by the silliest things. The little kid within comes bubbling to the surface and it's all over. Allow that belly laugh to blow and set a positive example of what's "normal" in your family.

Singing may prompt laughter as well, though the hilarity is unintended. Children love to guffaw at their parents almost as much as with them. Humor frees your children to join in on the fun. They see that Mom and Dad have their crazy moments too.

Crying can be tougher. Cultural or familial norms frequently prevent parents from appropriately emoting in moments of supreme sadness. When tragedy strikes, don't be afraid to let tears fall and sobs come. Your children may not fully understand, but they'll be touched because you are. They'll see that big boys and girls, like you, are sad sometimes. They will begin to develop empathy and compassion for others and a better understanding of their own emotional lows.

The Bible says even Jesus wept. Overcome with the sadness at losing a dear friend, He cried. But that's only one snapshot. At other times the Teacher joked. Help your children see the sparkle in His eye.

God made us to feel—to hurt, laugh, dance, sing, and smile. That's what living is all about. By allowing them to witness the whole gamut of adult intensity and emotion, you do your kids a huge favor. You put them in touch with their emotions and teach them when it's appropriate to let their feelings show—keys to a happy, well-adjusted life.

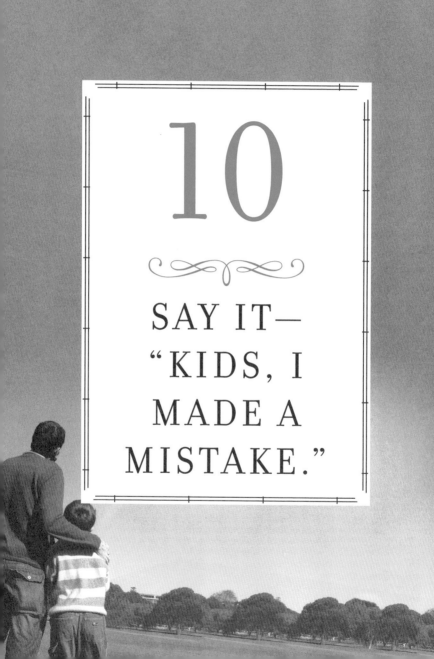

10

SAY IT—
"KIDS, I
MADE A
MISTAKE."

erfect parents don't exist. And if they did, would they be any fun? As it is, we pile mistake upon mistake and then add in a few more for good measure. If and when you blow it with your children, have the courage to tell them you were wrong. Practice now: "Kids, I made a mistake."

One of your greatest struggles will be to avoid bringing your personal battles, your "adults only" concerns home to your kids and then blaming them for becoming the trigger point. Have you ever lost your temper in a frustrating moment and lashed out at those you love? Almost every parent has. It's what you do next that makes all the difference.

When that occurs, you have a tremendous opportunity for your family to see humility in action. But be quick about it. The longer the lag between the offense and the admission, the weaker the impact of your words.

Confession may be the easiest part of the transaction. Without much prodding, we can launch into great detail about how we were "pushed" into our inappropriate response as our children listen wide-eyed. We blame others for our wrong reactions, responses we should have controlled. Stop. Rewind. Your kids are learning from your bad example.

When you blow it, no matter what your self-justification or backstory, move quickly beyond rationalizations to: "Please forgive me. I was wrong." It is only through offering yourself up to the mercy of your child that you can experience true reconciliation.

That rebonding pushes aside bitterness and quenches anger. 'Fessing up and asking for forgiveness short-circuits a debilitating pattern. Plus it provides your children with a model worth emulating in their relationships with both God and man.

11

SOAP DOWN YOUR CAR—ALL HANDS ON DECK

B ucket brigade front and center! Find a stack of clean rags, slip on shorts or swimsuits, and head outside for one of the most beloved chores known to childhood: washing the family car.

For parents, it's best to get your soaking over with all at once. Hand over the hose to the smallest member of the scrub-a-dub team and let him or her spray you from top to bottom. You'll keep cool, and the laughter level will jump off the scale. Then show them that turnabout is fair play in love and car washing.

When everyone's drenched, pass around the hose and fill up some soapy buckets and get to work. Include everyone who can toddle and heft a towel. Before you know it, the grime will be in the gutter.

The job is more fun if you sing silly songs together or put on a jumping-jolting music station and clean to the beat. Be careful or you may end up with the neighbors lining up to have their autos shined as well.

Working together to clean a car teaches a little something about true teamwork. Everyone has a task to do and each one is important, no matter how large or small the participant. Size makes no difference in God's eyes.

This simple task teaches your children that everyone in God's family has a certain calling, a responsibility to use their gifts for the greater good. At any age, they can and should put the needs of others above their own. Service opens the door to great accomplishments, no matter the size of the helper. What a life lesson—and it all started with an old garden hose.

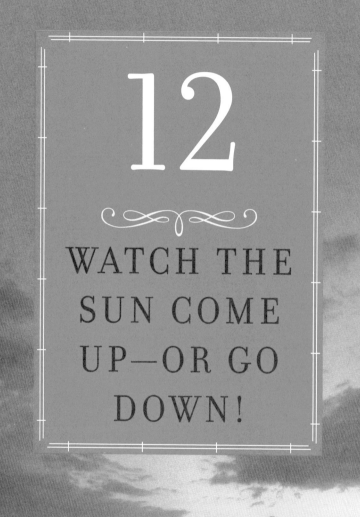

12

WATCH THE
SUN COME
UP—OR GO
DOWN!

K ids grow up so fast, one day running pell-mell into another. All the more reason to put on the brakes and take a look at the unrelenting, spectacular pageant of passing time— together.

Use the Internet to create a custom calendar with sunrise, sunset, and twilight times for your area. After choosing some optimal dates, pick a spot known for its breathtaking backdrop—maybe a sandy beach or a pull-off near a towering peak. No matter which location you choose, take along extra blankets for cool breezes, a few folding chairs, some snacks, and plenty of water.

Park safely off the road. Then unload and get your chairs situated for your own personal viewing of one of the most spectacular light shows on earth. The unfolding drama, the glimmering glow, the fireworks—take it all in. Notice how the sky transforms as the sun makes its move.

The regular movements of the sun should assure your children that God is the same moment to moment, day to day, and year to year. They won't have to worry about waking up to cold darkness, for God Himself set the sun on its perch above. Observe the exploding light rays, the bright oranges, golds, reds, and yellows.

God will send other beautiful mornings, other stunning nights, to give your children pure joy and delight. And every single shining scene will remind them of that time you all clearly saw God's finger painting the sky—a memorable moment in the unrelenting course of time.

13

TREAT YOUR KIDS TO "ONLY-CHILD" DATES

B rothers and sisters should be best friends. That's a given. But they still need time and space to themselves once in a while—or else they feel like one of the crowd instead of the unique individuals that they are. When you take time to treat each of your children as a person, not merely as one among many, self-esteem grows. They begin to feel secure in the fact that you love them simply for who they are.

A good way to express that one-on-one type of love is by taking your child out alone on a special date. It's a chance to better understand each child's unique personalities and interests. Even if you have only two children, it's easy to bundle them. You do whatever the louder of the pair demands. Until you separate out the sibling strands, you may not realize that one child's creativity has been stunted by the other's more forceful personality.

An "only child" date should be child-driven. Don't make assumptions. Ask your child to decide what he or she would like to do—see a movie, shop for shoes, go rock climbing, or take a horse-back ride—the list is as long as your child's imagination.

Add to the fun by following up your activity at a restaurant—once again, your child's choice. Allow plenty of time so you can talk of dreams and hopes, schemes and expectations. Take advantage of this rare chance to get a better glimpse of that sometimes stranger who lives in your home.

Whether you are young or old, the relationship you have with God is a one-of-a-kind experience. God wants to know your heart, feel your joy, and give you comfort. That's the same message you give your children when you make a special effort to treat them to the undivided attention they deserve.

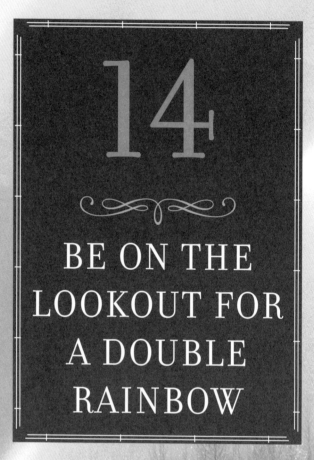

14

BE ON THE
LOOKOUT FOR
A DOUBLE
RAINBOW

D aily miracles often go unnoticed, especially now that television, video games, movies, and flashy electronics are vying for your kids' attention. Why not make it your goal to tune your kids in to the unique qualities of an extraordinary double rainbow?

Given their rarity, that could mean precious hours spent together waiting for the cherished event. Your kids will see that watching for miracles takes time and patience. While the anticipation builds, take every opportunity to describe the rainbow's layered blend of red, orange, yellow, green, blue, indigo, and violet and teach them to remember that combination by memorizing the Rainbow Man's name, Mr. R-o-y G. B-i-v.

Talk about how Old Man Noah was one of the first human beings to view a rainbow. About how that shining arch was God's promise that a flood would never again overwhelm the world.

Explain to your kids—while you're huddled together on the porch after a rainstorm—that double rainbows are visible only when raindrops high in the atmosphere refract and reflect light back to us. Encourage them to keep their eyes peeled because what you're looking for isn't an everyday, or every storm, occurrence. The color sequence of a secondary rainbow is switched, exactly opposite of the primary rainbow, making it truly unique.

Rainbows are fleeting treasures, transitory God sightings. And double rainbows are at least twice as priceless. Keep looking and eventually you and your children will be rewarded with a front-row seat to a stunning light show. When that happens, you will have an opportunity to marvel in wonder at the primary rainbow's reversed reflection, a remarkable double reminder of God's faithfulness.

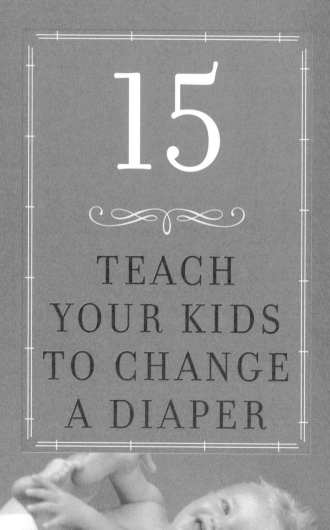

15

TEACH
YOUR KIDS
TO CHANGE
A DIAPER

Celebrate dirty diapers! Well, at least smile about them as you hold your nose. Messy diapers mean new life. Since the birth of a child is a full-fledged miracle, make a big deal of the occasion.

To help your children enjoy the excitement, pull out their own baby photos. Talk to your kids about how thrilled you were to hold them in your arms and how willingly you changed even the most dangerous diaper.

Of course, it helps if you have a baby of your own to practice on, but if you don't, there are always diaper-weary mothers who are willing to share the task with a responsible adult. If you come upon such an opportunity, take care to prep your children (no matter their ages) about which comments are appropriate and which aren't. Help them find kind words about the family's happiness, the infant's soft skin, and how cute the baby looks. Should a diaper change be required, see if the new parents will allow you to assist. The idea may delight them. Make a point of bringing your children to the changing table.

Emphasize how easy it is to change a diaper. Show them where to find the clean wipes, baby powder, and the trash can. After several chances to observe the operation, allow them to take over under your careful supervision. Diapering is a basic life skill that many young people never learn unless they have babysitting opportunities.

In a way, we are all like babies in need of a change and God offers to give us a good cleaning. He helps us pry our clasping fingers off the bulky baggage in our lives. Talk to your kids about how God gives them another chance even if they make a mess of things. Let the next dirty diaper serve as a potent object lesson!

16

CONDUCT
A LAUNDRY
SEMINAR

I f your kids think the laundry fairy slips clean clothes into their dresser drawers, maybe it's time for them to get a grip on the magic wands available in the utility room. Learning to do a load of wash without turning white shirts pink is a valuable life skill. You can have fun teaching your children the right way to launder their clothes by holding a "Welcome to Washing and Drying" seminar. To prepare, visit the Web site of your favorite laundry detergent for tips on doing a load right.

When you sense they're old enough (rule of thumb: when they can reach the knobs), issue the invitations for your class. Pass out paper and pencils for taking notes, and then pull out all the sprays, prewashes, detergents, and softeners. Going slowly so they can get it down on paper, introduce each product, explaining when and demonstrating how it is used.

From there, move on to the operation of the washer and dryer. Emphasize how to sort colors, how much is a load, how to set the gauges on both machines, and wind it all up with a demonstration of how to empty the lint filter. When you're ready to close, remind them that they should not hesitate to ask for help—preferably before the floor is covered with water.

A laundry chart with instructions for specific fabrics and colors is a nice way to remind your crew how to do each load properly. Post it above the washer along with a reminder that they are never to leave their clothes sitting in the washer or dryer for more than one hour.

Mom and Dad won't always be around to clean up stained shirts and messy dresses. Teaching your children to win at the laundry game offers them a step toward eventual independence.

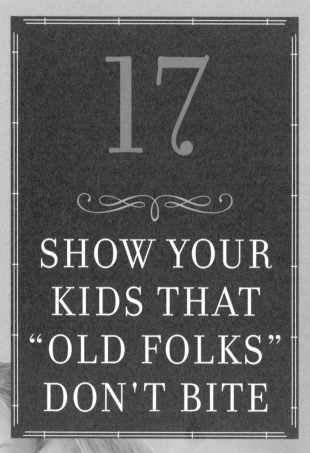

17

SHOW YOUR
KIDS THAT
"OLD FOLKS"
DON'T BITE

You've passed by countless times, maybe even wondered what it was like inside that well-tended white building. Certainly that nursing home is pretty on the outside, but are the residents really happy? You've probably never stopped to ask questions or find out how you might help. Here's your chance to change apathy to action and alter your child's perspective on "old folks" forever.

Within miles of your home live some of the brightest minds and saddest eyes you will ever encounter. Residents of nursing facilities are often lonely. The good intentions that friends and family had to stay in touch evaporate with the day-to-day grind, and they're typically delighted to learn that someone has taken the time to visit their loved one when they can't.

You and your children have an opportunity to become that friendly family fill-in at absolutely no cost. Make an appointment and go on a short-term joy-giver's trip. Many nursing homes welcome visitors, not just for Christmas caroling, but on weekends when the lack of family becomes most obvious. Check first and you may find that you're welcome to take along a gentle pet with you, another surefire solution for bringing back a spark of a smile.

You and your family can lighten the load of a lonely new friend—and give yourselves a special treat—by talking, listening, or sharing a picture, homemade card, or even a small gift. You're likely to meet some interesting characters who, when you're leaving, will cause you to wonder how soon you can come back.

The dividends for your kids will multiply simply because you decided to teach some young folks to treasure the elderly. Seeing these senior souls helps children rest in the thought that God is with them every step of their life's journey.

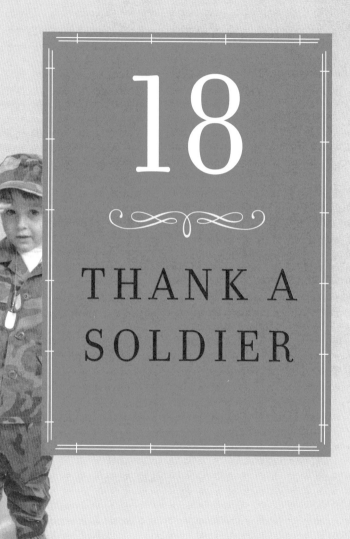

18

THANK A
SOLDIER

A grateful heart is one of the most valuable assets your kids can develop—but it isn't a characteristic that's easy to instill. Teenagers in particular often demonstrate great resistance to the idea of showing genuine gratitude. Don't let that cause you to back away from this important lesson. Instead, employ multiple strategies.

Begin by expressing your gratitude to God and to your spouse in front of your kids. Showing them is always better than telling them. Be sure to express your thanks to them as well. Greet even the smallest gesture with appreciation.

It's also important to let your kids see you thanking those outside your inner circle: those, for example, whose job it is to defend the common good—policemen, firemen, and expecially members of the military. With your kids in tow, take time to speak to a person in uniform, thanking that person for his or her personal sacrifices—time with family, physical safety, career goals, and financial gains. If your kids still aren't getting it, try organizing a yard or odd-job day for the family of a deployed soldier. Make sure they have an opportunity to meet the family personally and learn about their specific hardships.

Still another way to get your point across is to establish pen pal relationships for your kids with active members of the military. This can be done through letters and e-mail correspondence.

You may have to repeat these activities regularly before your kids understand the gravity of what is being done to protect their freedom and ensure their safety, but the result will be a priceless awakening of genuine gratefulness—one that will enhance their relationship with God and others and serve them well throughout their lives.

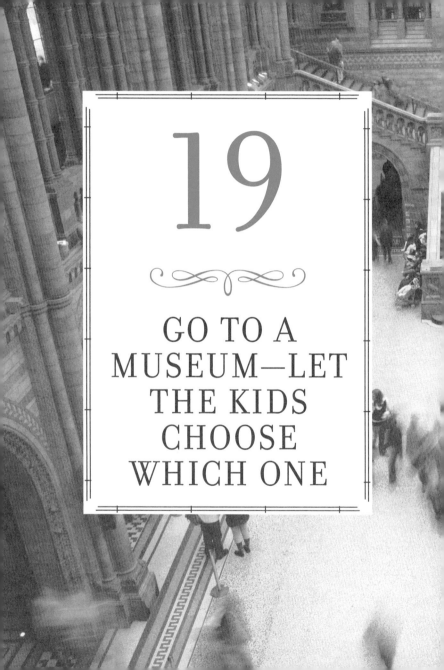

19

GO TO A MUSEUM—LET THE KIDS CHOOSE WHICH ONE

A trip to a museum should thrill both child and parent. Right attitudes could make it a life-changing adventure. To make the day more child-centered, let your own kids come to a consensus on which museum to explore. No matter how many times you go, you'll find something new to trigger the imagination. A call ahead will inform you of any special family programs or speakers of interest.

When you arrive, find a map of the exhibits, point out the restrooms and water fountains, and let the kids lead the way. Follow behind, watching. Kill the natural urge to direct the day.

You won't just learn about history, art, or science. You'll discover things you might never have noticed about your kids: what stimulates their thinking, what concerns them, what they'd like to know more about.

Expanding the mind begins with choices. The museum will offer many. When your child makes positive decisions about what interests (or doesn't interest) him, he shades in the outlines of his personality.

To add value to the experience, consider treating each child to a learning tool from the museum gift shop. Help them select a book or kit that will teach them even more about a new fascination and perhaps help curiosity flicker into flame.

God gave your children many gifts. As a parent you have a sacred duty to help them find which way He would have them grow. Ultimately, though, it's a decision they must own. A parent can make suggestions and offer direction, but at the day's end, your kids must be allowed to find their own paths and discover how best to use their very individual skills.

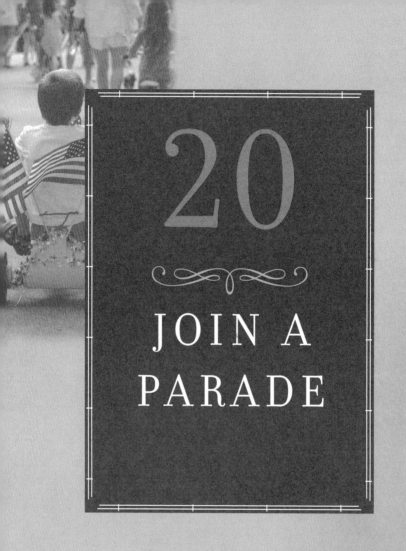

20

JOIN A
PARADE

E veryone loves a parade. The excitement, the precision, the rows of marchers—heads held high—strutting their stuff. Not only are they fun, but parades are prime opportunities to stand up, stand out, and show off. From clowns to convertibles to sequins and batons, a parade is a convergence of bombastic pride and exhibitionism. What a great way to give your kids a lesson in confidence and self-esteem.

Keep your eye out for a local celebration and then call to be sure all comers are invited to partake in the festivities. Walkathons and other fund-raisers are also a good place to make a positive contribution while having a great time. If all else fails, declare a Neighborhood Parade Day and enlist the ranks of every young marcher you can find.

Make preparation a family affair, giving suggestions for what each person will wear. Come up with a special parade chant or song, and you might even want to practice your Queen Elizabeth parade wave: palm out, fingers together, it's all in the wrist!

Maybe your event will merit a picture in the newspaper, but that shouldn't be the goal. The point is to forget about "what people will say" and simply get out there and have fun being yourself. Some teens may balk at first, but deep down they long to be in the lime-light. You may be surprised at their enthusiasm for making a statement in the street.

Being front and center with all eyes watching can help your kids overcome stage fright, excessive shyness, and a fear of standing out in the crowd. And isn't it really the goal of all parents to teach their kids to march to the drumbeat God's placed in their hearts and heads? You've just got to love a parade!

21

SPEND THE NIGHT IN THE ZOO

Ever heard a gorilla snore or watched elephants spray water on each other with their trunks? There's something about seeing the mighty lion, the graceful hippo, or the galloping giraffe that makes a trip to the zoo irresistible. Visiting the animals is an adventure that offers the chance to see the wacky results of God's amazing imagination. Let your children know that only He could create the wild and crazy animals who call the zoo "home."

But the fun doesn't have to stop when the doors to the public swing shut at night. The thrills are but beginning. Many zoos offer special overnight packages that allow kids the chance to snuggle in a sleeping bag next to a python—safely behind glass, of course. (The snake, that is—not your child!) They'll also enjoy good food and gentle lessons from the friendly zookeepers. Your kids will fall asleep in a setting they'll remember their whole lives. Contact your local zoo for information on these programs.

What child wouldn't love waking up to the sound of tigers rustling? Like you, they can't help wondering if the long-fanged critters have had their midnight snack already. Rest assured; they probably have. And if not, the staff might even offer your kids the chance to help with the feeding—under strict supervision, of course.

God didn't use up all His creativity on the birds and beasts. He had a generous dose left over for your child. A trip to the zoo teaches children that every giraffe has its own spotting pattern and each zebra has unique stripes. No two animals are exactly alike. Likewise, your zoo sleepover provides a tremendous opportunity to teach your children that they, too, are one-of-a-kind creations.

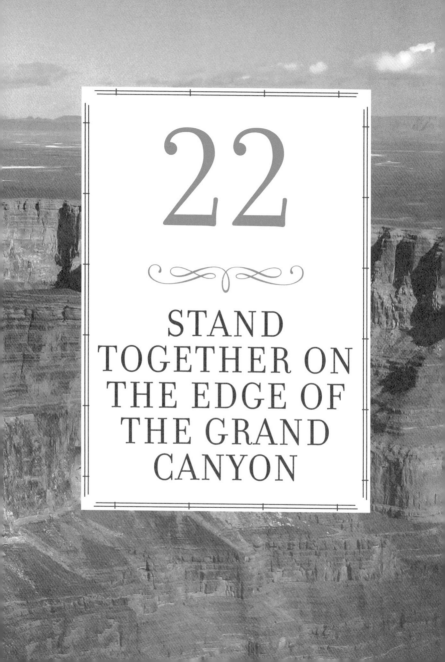

22

STAND TOGETHER ON THE EDGE OF THE GRAND CANYON

Not even a panoramic postcard can compare to a firsthand look into the depths of Arizona's Grand Canyon. This national park covers more than one million acres of land and sees well over five million visitors each year. (Kids between the ages of four and fourteen may be interested in the Junior Ranger programs. Check in at the Ranger Station in the park.)

Split in two by the Colorado River, the gaping canyon is a sight you and your children will never forget. Its walls are made of rocks and it has cliffs, ridges, hills, and valleys of every form and painted in a variety of unique hues. Sunsets and sunrises are spectacular both in the sky above the canyon and in the way the dancing light moves across its depths. It's like nothing you have ever seen before. *Breathtaking* is too mild an adjective to describe the awesome beauty.

Standing with your children, staring into the yawning mouth of this carved crevice, it's likely you'll feel tiny: like a mere water drop from a desert downpour—small and insignificant. Similarly, your kids may wonder at times if they'll ever accomplish great things.

But wait a minute. What if one drop joined two and two more join four? And so on. A roaring flood could soon appear, one powerful enough to tear away tons of dirt and rock. In fact, God used the natural force of erosion to cut away the remarkable Grand Canyon.

Like water drops that meld to form a raging river, the beautiful canyon reminds your kids that working together accomplishes miracles. Help your child go with God's flow. When you do, their inner beauty emerges and everyone will stand in amazement at the sculpture God reveals

23

INVITE A DOG,
CAT, GUINEA
PIG, OR BIRD TO
SHARE YOUR
DOMICILE

S hould you rename your backyard "Animal Planet"? Is there a zealous pet fanatic in your home? You know the type—the child who can't pass up a stray pup without leaning down to give it a pat and a long hug. Maybe you were once that child and still are at heart.

Kids and pets go together like peanut butter and jelly. Even if the kitten scratches the furniture or the doggy needs more practice making it outside in time, there's much to gain by making a permanent pet connection for your children. A guinea pig, fish, or bird can be full of personality if you take the time to communicate. Coax them out of their shells unless, of course, they're hermit crabs. Some claim it's even possible to train a cat to use a toilet! You won't know until you try.

It doesn't take long for pets to become members of the family. Every animal lover has a story about how his or her dog, cat, guinea pig, or fill-in-the-blank pet expressed intense affection when the owner was feeling the lowest.

Without doubt, animals are capable of exhibiting love, fear, pain, sadness, loneliness, and joy. Teach your child that God loves every animal, no matter how small. No animal should be viewed as disposable or "not worth the trouble."

Animal care teaches kids to take responsibility for another living thing—making sure their creature has fresh water, healthy food, and a clean place to sleep. Your children help guard God's worldwide zoo. In doing so, they begin to understand the bond between man and beast. They get a sense of why the Maker of the universe even keeps such careful track of a fallen sparrow.

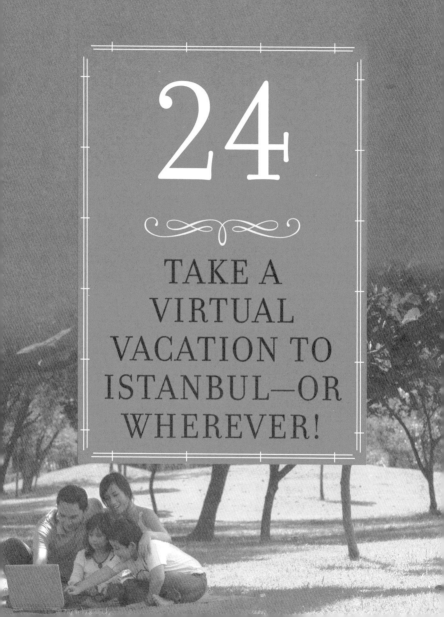

24

TAKE A VIRTUAL VACATION TO ISTANBUL—OR WHEREVER!

People once lived and died within miles of their birthplaces. They were confined for a lifetime to a couple of counties, a few square miles of space. That's no longer the case. Planes, trains, helicopters, and automobiles now take the adventurous countless miles abroad.

While travel may be easier today, there are still financial and personal restrictions that prevent most of us from winging our way over oceans and continents. With the advent of the Internet, though, the world awaits your fingertip touring. You and your children won't even have to get passports to discover what life's like in Istanbul—or anywhere else for that matter.

There's something exciting about stepping beyond your own borders to a place where the language, culture, history, and people are different. With the availability of virtual travel opportunities, you and your kids can sail the seven seas and never get wet. Type "Istanbul," for example, in your favorite search engine and you'll have a wealth of maps, photos, videos, and information waiting to explore.

The pleasure and safety of exploring the planet from the comfort of your home may inspire you. Perhaps your online adventures will help you prepare for the real thing one day. What a family vacation that could be!

While countries greatly vary in terms of customs, art, and even food, your children will discover the people of earth are more alike than different. As they travel over the Web to various destinations, they'll see similar needs: love, happiness, water, food, and other life essentials. They begin to realize God's love isn't simply for them, but for the whole family of man.

25

INVITE THE NEW FAMILY ON THE BLOCK OVER—AND LET THE KIDS COOK

Hospitality is a forgotten art. But it needn't stay that way. Help your kids get up the gumption to reach out to the new kids on the block. With some help and a little encouragement, they might find that extending themselves to those they don't know can be a pleasant and rewarding experience.

Go over to the new neighbors' home with your kids. Introduce yourselves and share a little bit of neighborhood folklore. Encourage your kids to meet their kids: no silent staring allowed. Keep it spontaneous and light. Conclude by asking the family to share a meal. If they accept, you're in business. Strangers often become friends over a simple meal prepared with love.

Back home, pull your kids into the menu-planning stage. You might want to make a quick call to check on food allergies or aversions. You'll then be able to give your children better direction about what they'd like to make. Yes, make.

Learning hospitality means more than showing up for a party and greeting your guests. The behind-the-scenes efforts can be substantial. Besides planning the meal, your children should shop with you for ingredients, come up with a fun centerpiece (stuffed animals, anyone?), decorate place cards, clean house, set the table, and—whew—before they know it, the company will be at the door.

God's Word talks about how people we meet may turn out to be angels in disguise. Imagine the look on your children's faces if that happened! But that shouldn't be your goal. Everyone feels lonely now and again, maybe even unwelcome. You and your kids can change all that. Making a stranger feel at home softens a child's heart to the needs of others. And if your guests turn out to be angels, next time ask them to bring the cake.

26

HAVE A TALK ABOUT DEATH AND HEAVEN

The only way to heaven is through death's door—a truth many of us balk at talking about. We'd rather not discuss what comes after we close our eyes for the last time. One day, though, each person will discover the truth about heaven firsthand. And as much as we might like to cocoon our kids, we can't hide this reality forever.

One day a grandparent, teacher, friend, or neighbor in your child's life will die. You'll then find yourself trying to instill hope and understanding in the midst of an emotional crisis. How much better to talk about this sensitive subject before reality comes knocking at the door.

Explain to your kids that death is inevitable, but so is life eternal. At our appointed times God calls us home, and a new adventure begins. We'll see Him face-to-face, ask a few questions, and finally understand some of the mysteries we've struggled with here on earth. Read passages from the Bible, such as John 14, where Jesus prepared His disciples for His death. Let them know that death is little more than temporary separation for those who trust in Christ.

Years fly by. The older we get, the more we realize that we're but one thin layer between our children and eternity. As time rolls on, they'll lose their great-grandparents, grandparents, and then us.

From God's perspective, our lives barely sprint past the starting line and are over. Fortunately, He has created a home for everyone who trusts in Him, a glorious shining place where fears and tears are banished and death has no power, a place where reunions happen every few seconds and hearts are forever free. Heaven: where timeless time begins.

27

SING THE FAMILY SONG—OVER AND OVER AND OVER

Every family needs a favorite song. Be it "Row, Row, Row Your Boat" or "Have You Ever Seen a Lassie?" kids love singing simple songs. Over and over and over. Think about your last car trip. Assuming eyes were at attention and headphones pulled off, you could have sung "Hush Little Baby" to quiet a howling infant, "On Top of Spaghetti" to stave off prelunch hunger pangs, and "For He's a Jolly Good Fellow" to keep the driver awake.

An especially musical crew might come up with a personal family song. Just take a familiar tune and add amusing words of your own. Have the official family secretary jot them down because spur-of-the-moment creativity can slip away before being committed to memory.

If writing original lyrics seems a bit much, pull out a folio of old favorites. Or sing along to any number of collections of children's music. You'll hear perky singers wailing on "Muffin Man," "London Bridge Is Falling Down," "Yankee Doodle," "Farmer in the Dell," "Skip to My Lou," and more. Before long, you'll have a whole repertoire of kiddie classics to choose from to make the next family road trip seem a little bit shorter.

Singing releases a grand giddiness, a buoyant spirit in children of any age. That's why it's so much fun. And even if critics would classify your joyful noise as "croaking," persevere.

You and your kids don't have to be opera prima donnas to enjoy a family song. Even those who can't carry a tune in a bucket can sing along and enjoy a memorable time of family fun and bonding.

28

MAKE EVERY FAMILY AFFAIR A PHOTO OP

S ay cheese! Time for that candid camera to make its dreaded appearance. When was the last time you put in a roll of film or fired up the digital camera and snapped everyone in sight? Silly faces, funny poses, bunny ears behind heads? Anything goes.

If you need some help with the basics, visit *www.kodak.com* for tips on taking great pictures. Here's one guarantee: Place your kids front and center in the photo, squat to shoot at eye level, and you're on the way to great portraits.

To avoid an overdose of perfect plastic smiles or prevent squinting, poking, pinching, or crying, forget about formal poses. Photograph life as it happens and enjoy the results, whatever they may be. If you relax, so will they.

Large family events provide an opportunity to create an archive of friends and families for your kids. Enlist them to help make grown-ups smile and coax grumps into grins. They'll love being shoulder to shoulder with the photographer for a change. Assign one person to make sure the new pictures are complete by adding names and dates to the backs. That little exercise will save lots of guessing later.

The truth is, we wake up with bed head and morning breath. Sometimes we push our kids and ourselves to keep up with all the other seemingly flawless families. We're just wasting our time. After all, our kids see us without masks.

So help them stop worrying about exceeding the ideal by being the cutest, sweetest, best-dressed kids that ever graced a frame. God accepts us flaws and all. So does a loving family. You don't have to be perfect to bask in God's love and neither do your children.

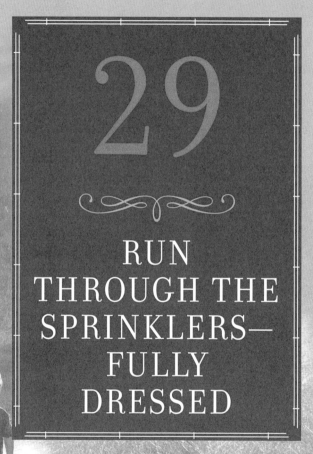

29

RUN THROUGH THE SPRINKLERS— FULLY DRESSED

On your mark. Get set. Sprinkle!

If you're cautious, you can take your wallet out or check your purse at the door before you jog through the jiggling streams of water. Otherwise wear some washable play clothes and go for the flow. Begin by walking slowly toward the water hand in hand with your kids, everyone trying to guess which splish will splash you first—and where!

Once you're over the initial shock, just go for it. Take turns running through the wavy spray. Help your youngest jumper make the leap over the sprinkler. Don't stop at only one pass, though; leap and cavort with your kids until you are all completely soaked.

Your children will be stunned and amazed at the silliness. And they'll be delighted that you actually came up with such a cool plan. It's unexpected, it's fun, and leaves your kids wondering: "What in the world will they think up next?"

The point of this dramatic dash? To teach your kids to be ready for anything. We can't and don't know from day to day which of our plans will (and maybe should) change. Only God knows. And sometimes His ideas about what is best for us make as much sense to our human minds as tearing through the sprinklers fully dressed.

That's part of the adventure of life for you and your kids. God's plans often involve what you would never expect. When you obey and follow anyway, you discover new things about yourself—wonderful things. So will your children. As with the sprinkler dash, they'll discover what it feels like to be cool and refreshed, soggy and smiling, ready for whatever may be coming their way next.

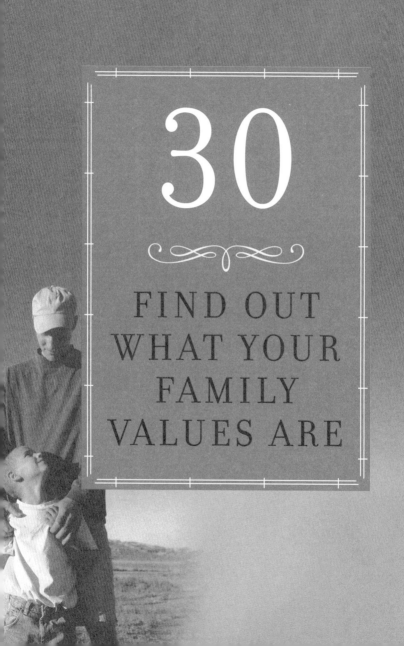

30

FIND OUT
WHAT YOUR
FAMILY
VALUES ARE

Politicians put on their sparkly family values hat whenever an election approaches. You and your kids will hear about how Mr. or Ms. So-and-So feel that "much more" should be done to "strengthen the family" (whatever that means).

But when you're in the trenches trying to make ends meet, family values take on a whole different meaning. You do without so your kids can have a new pair of shoes. You take on an extra shift to pay for Christmas gifts. You give up your leisure time to help out with home- work. You willingly put your children's needs before your own.

Children understand that you care when you spend time with them, listen to their questions, and meet their needs. Putting them first squeezes out your own selfishness. There isn't room if you truly value your kids. They know that you'll be there to help them when they need it because you want what's best for them—which doesn't necessarily equate with what makes them happy.

It's a paradox. Kids sense the great divide between parents who say the right things and those who back up their words with actions. That's what the term "family values" really means: "I love you" combined with necessary firmness. No parent enjoys laying down the law, but without your willingness to do the right thing even if it's tough, your children will know you're full of processed lunch meat, not a parent who means what you say.

Putting your children first teaches them to put others first. So take the "treat others as you'd like to be treated" rule and apply it liberally to your kids. They'll feel valued in God's eyes if they know they're valued in yours.

31

GET ELBOW-
TO-ELBOW
OVER A 1000-
PIECE PUZZLE

Eighteen thousand: that's the number of pieces in one of the most complex and frustrating jigsaw puzzles on the market today. Committed puzzle addicts drool at the prospect. Tell your kids you decided to go easy on them and purchase only a one-thousand-piece mystery to solve.

Set aside a table dedicated to the puzzling process. That gives you a chance to work for a time and then give it a rest when you get googly-eyed. You and your children will go through spells of frenzied excitement as the pieces come together quickly and utter disgust when you seem to sit for hours without finding a single match. Here's a hint: teach your kids to sort by colors and always build the border first to provide an edging to your masterpiece.

Though it doesn't look like it until the very last pieces go in, the puzzle will finally come together. And while you're waiting for that to happen, you've got a perfect opportunity to talk to your kids about all kinds of issues without the intensity of a staged conversation. You're just there, heads together, getting the job done—if a conversation breaks out, it's a gift, a blessing.

The wonderful thing about puzzling is that it engages the brain without cluttering the mind. It holds on to your attention while freeing your thoughts. It's one of the few shared activities that actually encourage interaction between the players. All the more reason to make it a coming together spot for spontaneous give-and-take.

So . . . pull up the chairs, open the box, and pour out the pieces. It's time to get eyeball-to-eyeball with those kids of yours.

32

❦

HUG YOUR
KIDS UNTIL
THEY LET GO

E ver had a one-way hug? It happens to all of us. You can't wait to greet friends or family members. You put your arms around them hoping for a warm response. Instead their limbs hang limp in bored "Are you through yet?" body language. The rejection makes you feel like crawling back under the covers. And for parents, it can be a common experience.

When your kids are young, they may squirm to get free and play. And you may go through a barren time when hugs are few and far between during your kids' teen years. But every once in a while, your child will need a little more. You'll feel the hug around your neck go on and on. And you'll realize that your child has come shoulder to shoulder with the realization that parents are a rich source of the comfort and assurance they so badly need. Kids will also feel freer if they see you and your spouse hugging each other. You set the pace—set a good example. You might even want to make hugging a habit expected before leaving the house in the morning or going to bed at night.

When hugs happen, treasure them as the gifts they are. And whatever you do, don't let go until they do. Let your kids set the pace. Simply love them. Don't rush them, bug them, or beg them. God doesn't work that way and neither should you.

Hugs can't be forced. When they are, the joy and spontaneity disappears. But there are special moments when you're glad to be a parent. Nothing beats the thrill of a breathtaking bear hug that seems to go on forever.

33

MAKE A BIG PRODUCTION!

Picture it: your children dressed as frolicking felines as you come forward to belt out "Memories" as only you can. You and your spouse play Shakespeare's star-crossed lovers, Romeo and Juliet, with the kids working the lights and humming gentle background music. Or maybe you just act out an extremely abbreviated version of *War and Peace* with puppets.

You and your kids are bound only by the limits of your imagination and your willingness to tap into your God-given talents. You can find screenplays, folios, and scenes for actors at the library. Let the kids help make a final selection.

Another option is to play "The Lonely Goatherd" song from *The Sound of Music* (or a favorite clip from any movie) until you've memorized your parts. Then have at it. Mix and match costumes from the dress-up box, find the props you need, and you're ready.

Before you call the press, though, put in the necessary practice time. Even an off-off-off-Broadway production requires dedication. Run your lines until everyone has them down pat. Younger kids can memorize as well as anyone, and you may discover you have a real drama king or queen on your hands.

Take the time to work on expression, emoting, and enunciation. Keep it light and fun, but let your kids realize there's work involved in the breezy, easy banter they see in films and plays. Your children will see that sometimes things go wrong with the show.

In real life, bad timing hurts feelings and causes confusion. God often puts people in scenes they didn't orchestrate. Whether at school or work, your young actors will have to go with the flow, to improvise. God will help your kids write their script and they'll shine brightest if they take their cues from Him.

34

CONQUER A
MOUNTAIN

Climb every mountain—or at least one tough one. Take your kids to the library and find your state map. Show them the elevation of the peaks. Then pick one nearby and set a goal: climb Mount Tippy-Top by the end of the summer.

Pick a location that meets your family's age, health, and climbing abilities. A hike may be all you can handle at first. It'll take some time to work your way up to Mount Everest! Set small goals like walking together to the corner store. When you get there, buy everyone a treat.

Explore online resources or check out mountain-climbing books from your local library. Talk with your kids about the challenge before them. Teach about climbing hazards, beasts and bugs to beware of, first aid, and equipment checks. You'll also want to investigate weather conditions to be sure you have the necessary gear.

Before you take one step up that steep incline to the top, walk regularly around your block—a great opportunity to talk and to build up stamina and strength. Be sure to work in those new shoes before you tackle the peaks. Your kids will enjoy the training best if they have plenty of breaks, snacks, and reasonable expectations. Set goals and give regular rewards so your kids build up their muscles. When you finally reach the top, take a picture of the proud mountaineers.

God gives us many mountains to climb, some by choice and others by default. Kids who have the confidence to scale a towering peak will find themselves more than able to tackle the struggles of life, no matter where the challenges rise.

35

DANCE
TOGETHER IN
THE OCEAN
WAVES

Water is unstoppable. It can seep through the smallest pinprick and burst a dam. Video clips of mountain-tall tsunamis show the power and intensity of an uncontrolled flow. Even ocean waves change with the seasons, triggered by solar and lunar gravitational pulls.

When the season and the weather permit, invite your kids to step into the wet with you. Feel the splash, smell the brine, and hold hands as you prance and dance in the billowing waves. It's wonderful fun.

Show your younger children how to draw a picture in the soft, wet sand and watch the surf inch up and erase it. Then engage them in a search for seashells—all shapes and sizes. They make great souvenirs of your day at the beach.

Stronger swimmers may feel comfortable going out farther, but help your younger children stay secure by remaining in shallow water. Kick up the water and splash until you're laughing. Do-si-do and around you go. If you tumble into the spray, come up laughing. A gentle, lolling seashore on a sunny day can make anyone forget the storms that sometimes batter the coastline.

Dancing with your children in the waves gives a new perspective. Point out to sea, where the water seems to stretch impossibly far; talk about how tiny you are. Yet remind them that God has His eyes upon you as you dance and laugh together in the sunshine.

When we jump, twirl, spin, and whirl in His wildness, we find a place of peace. Sometimes a wall of water can come along to knock us down. Teach your children to be thankful that His hands hold them safely even amidst the somersaulting waves of the unpredictable sea of life.

36

EXPLORE THE
BACKYARD
WITH A
MAGNIFYING
GLASS

I magine looking at your shoe from a bug's-eye view—a huge clomper crashing down. Someone yells, "Run!" and the anthill bubbles over. There's a lot to see when you take to the jungle outside your screen door. You and your young explorers need to be on the alert for tiny creatures. And no matter what the ants say, wear boots or shoes.

Find a powerful magnifying glass or two and head out on safari. Take along your imagination, and knee pads for Mom and Dad might be a good idea too. You'll be amazed at the sights awaiting discovery in your backyard.

Help small children find a place where they can view miniscule animal acrobats. Hunt for insects under rock edges and beneath old boards. But be careful. You're guaranteed success in your quest. You might stumble upon a snake or another unwelcome slitherer. And be wary of ants, which are fond of getting into pants.

If you have a muddy patch out back, use your magnifying glass to track paw prints of cats, foxes, squirrels, or an occasional raccoon. Do research on the Internet or at the library with your kids to find out more about tracking techniques. You might be surprised at the kinds of creatures sneaking around in your yard.

There's more to see than animals. Turn your lens on intricately designed leaves, a stiff blade of grass, and a sparkly rock. You'll be amazed at the detail. Explore the soft, colored trails within a blooming rose. God's craftsmanship comes through with astonishing clarity.

When you first stepped out the door, you weren't really looking. Then you opened your eyes to discover much more of the world in your backyard. Tiny life, tiny details abound. Slow down with your children to take a second look. Sometimes that's all it takes to see a whole new world.

37

PICK UP
TRASH IN
A PARK

Yuck." That's likely to be the reaction of your neatniks when you announce Cleanup Day at the Park. Other kids, the ones who carefully examine every piece of trash they find, will take to the task like bears to honey. Provide standard-issue plastic bags and have them wear garden gloves in case they come upon something sharp or rusty. Turn toward the park and march.

Along the way, you'll see cigarette butts, twist ties, fast-food containers, and more. Who knows? Let your kids get into the swing of things by snatching up trash en route. Pretty soon you'll have a healthy competition going. Who can fill up his or her bag the quickest?

No matter how hard you try, though, you'll never clean the whole park. Set a time limit so your kids can play after their labors. Ask them why people toss their trash on the ground instead of into garbage cans. They might suggest that people are sloppy, lazy, or didn't mean to make such a mess. Perhaps the polluters think someone else will come along to clean up.

That may be the simplest explanation. And that's why some pristine forests look like restaurant parking lots and clear mountain lakes turn brown. One person's tiny addition to the pile won't tip the scales, right? It might. Thankfully, one family can make a huge difference when it comes to making things better.

Disposing of someone else's junk can be a pain. But someone has to do it or the situation gets worse. Remind your kids that they have become part of the solution rather than part of the problem. Even if no one else notices, God will.

38

❦

SERVE IN
A SOUP
KITCHEN

Most meals find us eating until we're full and beyond. Why stop before it's gone? Your own munchers may serve as the poster family for the "eyes are bigger than the stomach" habit. If that's the case, help your children gain a better grasp on their gullets by encouraging them to step into a world where a hot meal is a luxury and going to sleep hungry is too often the norm. Call a local soup kitchen and ask if you and your family can spend a day helping out with whatever needs to be done. You won't be turned away.

The people who come for food often have no viable alternatives. They lack funds to buy a meal but their children need to eat. Your own kids may be shocked to see others their age in line. Although they dress differently, they're the same hungry crowd you'd see at school. They just need a little extra help right now.

That's why you're there. Have your children serve food or set tables. Encourage them to strike up conversations; show them how. The Bible says we should share with our needy neighbors (Deut. 15:7–8) and never feel more privileged or deserving. That's a key concept and a simple one. God loves us, and He doesn't want any of His children to go hungry. He is, after all, the Bread of Life.

By helping make a meal for someone else a reality, your children will gain a new perspective on their store of snacks in the cupboard. Grateful or not, they live in a home of plenty. God wants them to share what they have—be it food, time, or money—and rejoice in the chance to fill the emptiness of someone in need.

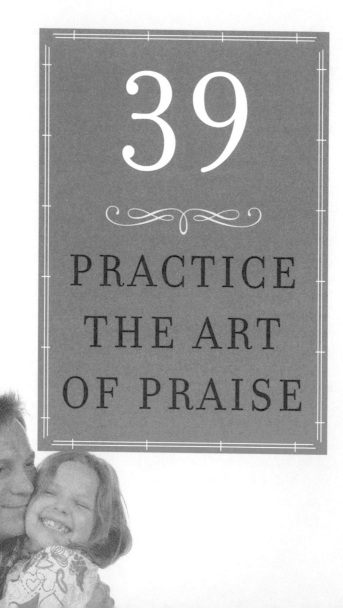

39

PRACTICE
THE ART
OF PRAISE

A kind word is like a priceless gem kept below the blankets at the back of a packed closet: worthless if hidden. When you horde nuggets of praise, you deprive your children of the opportunity to learn that it's as delightful to give encouragement as it is to receive it. Praise-giving delights the heart.

Sadly, many parents grew up in homes where encouraging words were kept tightly boxed under lock and key. For whatever reason, you may have been denied that "Great job!" or "Way to go!" that would have meant so much to you. Today you have amassed amazing accomplishments and yet feel your achievements are unnoticed. Your kids might feel the same way. Turn inside-out the pattern of disinterest. Give your kids the good words they deserve.

Remind them that God sees and cares too. Their heavenly Father rejoices at every triumph even if you can't be there. As parents you have the privilege of giving kids the tangible touch of gentle words. When you uplift and encourage, they can reach heights they never imagined.

So open your eyes to their wonderful gifts and talents. Then string together bright thoughts to form strands of praise. Watch these jeweled creations stretch and expand. Soon your kids will start building some of their own praise strands to give away. Tell your children when they've done a great job making their beds, helping with dinner, or completing their schoolwork.

Opportunities are boundless when you look for ways to say, "Well done. You're a terrific kid." You, too, will have a reward when you walk the shiny path of praise and hear your children calling you "blessed." But it all begins with you.

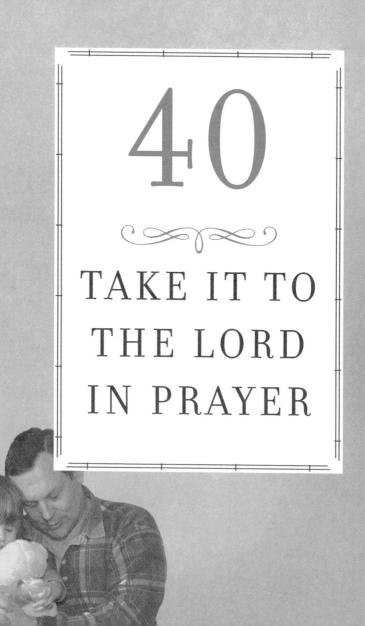

40

TAKE IT TO THE LORD IN PRAYER

Prayer is potent. How many lives have been lengthened and strengthened because people have dropped to their knees to ask for God's help for themselves or others? Hardened hearts have crumbled, the weakest have become mighty, and little children have changed the world. All through prayer.

When you and your children pray, you finally stop trying to solve problems alone. You talk out difficulties with God and count on Him to answer. No matter what you're facing, He understands. It's up to you to ask, however, and then patiently wait for the reply.

Should you hear that someone's sick or learn of a car accident, pause to pray. Pray first and often. There will be plenty of time to rush into action but only one initial opportunity to get your mind focused on the Problem-Solver. You need His help, so ask for it.

Your children should hear prayers outside of rote offerings at meals and bedtimes. When they come to you with a problem, pray. Is there a big event coming up, an exam at school? Ask if you can pray with them. No pressure. No fancy words. Just a simple "Hey, let's ask for God's help, shall we?"

The next time you feel hurt or confused, ask them to pray for you. Hold hands. They will see your heart, your vulnerability, and your reliance on God and follow suit. Some days you go to God with hair afire in Level Ten Crisis Mode. Slowly breathe prayers in and out. Teach your kids to turn to Him when the problem arises, not after it's a tangled mess.

If your children hear you handle difficulties by praying, they'll do the same. They'll learn that, like you, they can't do it all themselves. Fortunately, God is there and hears their heartfelt prayers.

41

~·~

CONDUCT
A WORKSHOP
ON CAR
MAINTENANCE

L et's see a show of hands: who knows how to repair your car's transmission or overhaul your engine? If so, go directly to the last paragraph, pull out your wrenches, and dive under the hood with your kids. For the rest of us, here are some simple, easy-to-follow tips for keeping your car running smoothly.

Think G-O-B: gas, oil, brakes. Let your kids learn how to put gas in the car, top off the tank, and pay for the purchase. Show them how to pull out the dipstick—on level ground after the car has had time to cool—and read the oil level. Teach them to add a quart when the level's low. Be sure you take them with you when you have your mechanic check the brakes. If you hear that shrieking sound signaling brake trouble, point out the problem so your kids can learn from the lurching.

When you stop for gas, have your children clean the windows and show them how to check the tire pressure. Soon they'll be reminding you when these basics need attention. You should also have them go through a checklist to make sure you have on hand maps, an emergency flare, a first-aid kit, extra water, and some simple tools. Search online for free maintenance tips and ideas for improving car travel with kids.

Car maintenance helps prevent car trouble—the unexpected kind that could leave your kids stranded on the side of the road or in an accident. It's one more way you can help your kids stay safe. And imagine what all that car information will be worth to them when they get their own wheels. Believe it—they'll thank you later.

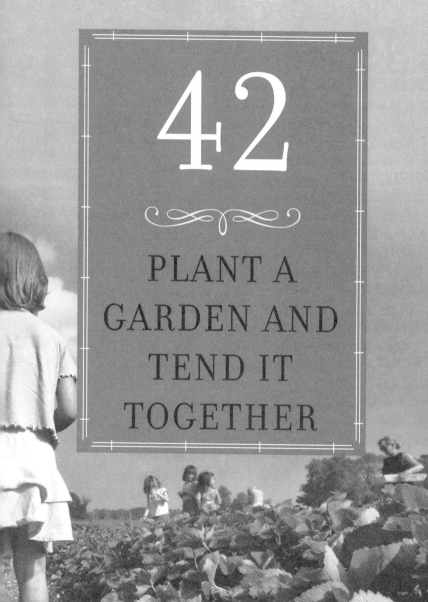

42

PLANT A
GARDEN AND
TEND IT
TOGETHER

R oses are red and pretty: it's true.
 But if food's what you want, a garden's for you.
 Gardeners know a secret: growing groceries is fun.
Whether you simply plant a passel of strawberry plants or a few
lines of peas or beans, or dig up all your grass and put in a farm,
you and your children will discover together the miracle of the seed
and the power of patience.

Even the smallest city lot or apartment has room for a planter of
herbs. To grow more, consider square-foot gardening. According
to *squarefoot.com*, this requires very little space and uses 80 percent
less water than conventional gardening. You can harvest a crop with
a plot as small as four feet by four feet. This all-natural planting
method requires no thinning, few seeds, and gives the most food
for the time invested. You may want to include marigolds to keep
pests away. For this purpose also consider planting onions, garlic,
daffodils, tulips, lavender, and mint.

As you open up the seed packages, show your children how tiny
the plants' beginnings are and how few seeds are contained in a
package. After you've buried the seed, remind your kids that you've
done your part—the rest is up to God. The same is true when we
take our problems to Him. We leave them in His care and then we
wait patiently. God often works in secret, but when we trust Him,
we can see miracles happen.

The moment someone spots green tips of growth, gather
around. Keep watering, weeding, and waiting. Make a special meal
of the harvest. Thank God for providing all good things, including
the tiny seeds that grow into a feast fit for the King's kids.

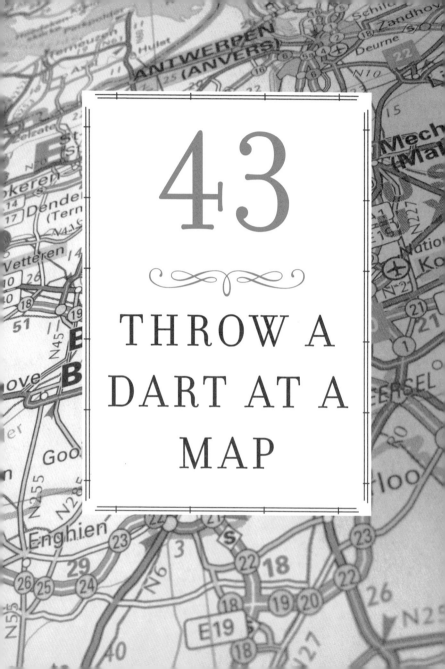

43

THROW A DART AT A MAP

A cross town or around the world—you pick the map and toss a dart. Then take a trip with the kids to discover more about your randomly chosen "hot spot." There's a wealth of fun and relaxation available even in the smallest community. Go online to find some of the craziest attractions imaginable. Then consider exploring them in person.

Make a long weekend or full-blown adventure out of a dart throw. Include your children in the planning. As with any trip, take along books, games, and audios for the car. Be sure to take plenty of breaks and have snacks and water on hand.

Once you arrive, find a place to share a meal. Ask a local for restaurant suggestions. You may stumble upon a small bakery or used bookstore that becomes a favorite hangout. Locate the must-see sights, keeping eyes open especially for free tours and samples. Find out all you can about the town or city you're visiting. Take a look at any historical homes or buildings, noting the architecture. Every place is unique and discovering what makes it so can be great fun.

Above all, relax. Make stress-free fun the doctor's orders. And if you aren't near a national monument, settle for gobbling down Tiny Town's Largest Pancakes. With the right attitude, you're sure to find both fun and good times.

As with any trip, things will go wrong, but you and your children should see the bumps in the road as colorful events that make your trip unforgettable. A big, wide, wonderful world is out there ready to be explored. What are you waiting for?

44

⌘

STRIKE UP
A FAMILY
BAND

A waken the grand band hidden in your home. With a little work, you and your kids can make music even if you're not ready to film a music video. To create a family band, mix fun-loving hearts with the sincere desire to better appreciate music.

If your kids have some inherent musical ability and can keep the beat, provide toy instruments and see how you sound. Consider buying plastic recorders at a music store. You can pick them up for a song. If your children are older and with music lessons under their belts, look for ways to play a simple special number together. If you visit *www.thefamilycorner.com*, you can find out how to make nine inexpensive musical instruments. Once you've chosen your weapon, work on a song together until you all recognize the melody.

Option two involves assigning everyone an instrument sound. Let each make their best impression. Someone conducts and then randomly points to each person. You won't believe what you have. Try "Mary Had a Little Lamb" or some other popular classic and have each child make their appointed noise when they get the point of the conductor's wand. Fun's guaranteed even if the song flops.

Finally, become a famous family air band with a CD recording of Vivaldi's *Four Seasons* or Bach's "Brandenburg Concerto." Line up the chairs and go through the motions of chugging on a tuba, fingering a flute, or pounding on a piano. You'll have a blast and your children will learn that making beautiful music takes both time and a whole lot of practice.

You don't have to be a world-class musician to lead your own family band. Have fun with it!

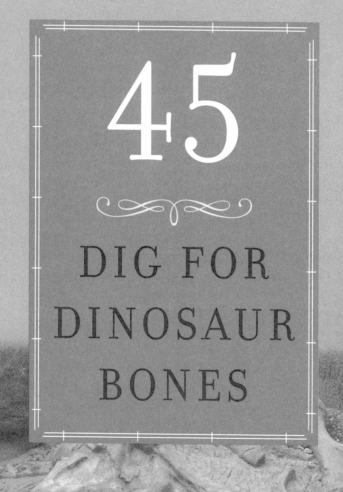

45

DIG FOR DINOSAUR BONES

Dinosaurs are kid magnets. You can find the ancient crea-tures on pillowcases, lamps, and even squished into edible gummy shapes.

Why are children of all ages so enthralled? Because dinosaurs are first and foremost a mystery. We have no photos or videos of these enormous beasts, just digitalized montages. And despite the movie myths projected as facts, no one knows exactly what they looked like, sounded like, or acted like. Paleontologists are more than happy to make guesses, but no one can be positive. If your child draws a picture of a purple polka-dotted monster breathing fire, encourage that creativity. Who knows? Maybe he's right.

There are come-one, come-all dinosaur digs and exhibitions going on throughout America and the world—Dinosaur, Colorado, for one. Montana is another hot spot for old bones. If you live close enough, you can make a day of actually digging for the real thing. Denver's Dinosaur Ridge—an outdoor museum—is also a great option. Or you can visit the Dinosaur Museum in Blanding, Utah, where you and your kids will have an opportunity to see dinosaur skeletons, fossilized skin, eggs, even footprints.

Search online for details of various archaeological adventures you and your family could consider. Though costly, these once-in-a-lifetime events are ones your kids will never forget.

Finding dinosaur bones is like finding buried treasure. To many scientists, it's better. Learning about things that happened once-upon-a-time-ago provides answers to questions we have today. Talk to your children about how the Bible tells the story of the earth's creation. As you look at experts digging up bones either on site or online, read Genesis 1:1. God created everything—even the amazing thunder lizards from the past.

46

START A PILLOW FIGHT

D eclare war on your kids. Feather pillows work best, but any soft bundle of fabric-covered fluff will do. Ready, set, go! Whack away wildly. Anything goes in love and pillow fights. Well, almost.

Pause that picture of feathers floating in slow-mo. Take a couple of steps back in time. First, find a suitable room and remove any obvious breakables. Take pictures off the walls, put foam over pointy head- and footboards, and warn all participants about potential impediments to fun. Be sure everyone understands the ground rules of civilized pillow fighting. Announce that the pillow must leave the tosser's hands. You cannot hang onto the edge of your fluffy weapon and keep flailing away at your victim. Pillows are projectiles so use them as such. Beware that smaller kids (and bigger ones) can get hurt if you're not careful.

The object of this exhibition is innocent silliness. Think of it as an indoor snowball fight without the cold, ice, or mittens. What could be better? So let the pelting begin! And one more thing: Let the young ones win—at least some of the time. See firsthand the delight in a child's eyes when he lobs a pillow across the room and gets you in the kisser.

What's to be gleaned from such gleeful goofiness? Pillow fights help your kids get it through their heads that parents were kids once. You may no longer look like a child of eight, but when you try, you can act like one. Maybe you begin to feel again what your children are going through. A good old-fashioned ruckus relieves tensions and brings old memories to life while making some great new ones.

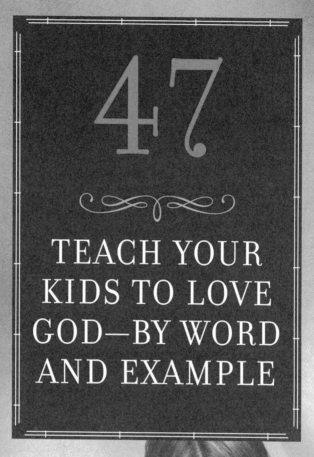

47

TEACH YOUR KIDS TO LOVE GOD—BY WORD AND EXAMPLE

E ven adults have trouble grasping the concept of God. In some ways He's like the wind, unseen but clearly there. His force can be felt. So can His love. You have the opportunity to help your children understand more about their Creator and why He's worthy of their adoration.

Young observers learn of the nature of God when they see you respect and revere Him. Your children won't believe your words unless your talk matches the way you live your life. Families get stuck in the routine rut of run-of-the-mill religiosity. You attend church, recite prayers, and do the same things all over the next week. That's not enough unless you're fulfilling God's purposes. Deep down no one buys it. You and your kids hate going through the motions (or are so numb you don't even notice). The only answer is to keep it real.

Tear down the façade. Be open about your need for God, your love for Him, and how much you rely on Him. Let your kids see your relationship with God, complete with the blemishes. Who likes admitting they're weak and needy? But we are. Children, with all their questions and challenges, only serve to pound in the point more deeply. Your children should see that God matters in your life. And that you put Him first.

That's done by reading His Word, and by praying and studying. Don't make a show of it; just be consistent. Soon, you'll see them following your lead. Loving God can mean putting your goals and dreams on hold to accomplish His plans. As parents you know exactly the cost of such love. And your sacrifices daily teach your kids what true love means.

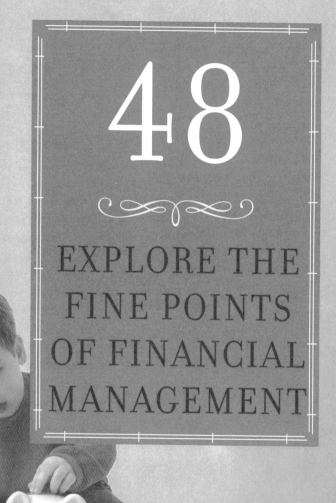

48

EXPLORE THE FINE POINTS OF FINANCIAL MANAGEMENT

*M*oney management. Sounds ominous, doesn't it? But it isn't really all that tough to teach your children good financial principles, and doing so will serve them well throughout their lives. Begin when they're old enough to understand the purpose of money. Train them to spend some, save some, have fun with a little, and give some to God's work.

The saving part comes first. If they get a dollar, place a dime in a piggy bank. That's long-term savings—not to be touched. Put another dime into a jar to give to a church or ministry. Every few months, let the kids decide where that should be donated. Take a third dime for little extras: candy, the movies, or other completely frivolous possibilities. This "mad money fund" lets them have a little fun within their budget while protecting the primary nest egg. Finally, put the other seventy cents into a jar for them to spend for things they both need and want. This simple formula works, whether for one dollar or one thousand.

When they're old enough, help them open savings and checking accounts. Show them how to create a written budget, save for purchases they really want, give to those less fortunate, and balance a checkbook.

Your efforts will carry much more weight as your kids see you managing your own finances well—regardless of whether you have plenty of money or barely enough to get by. It will make a strong impression if they see you spending wisely, putting money away in savings, and giving to those in need.

Unless your kids are planning to hide away in a monastery somewhere, money is and will continue to be a constant in their lives. While you still can, make sure they know how to make it work for them.

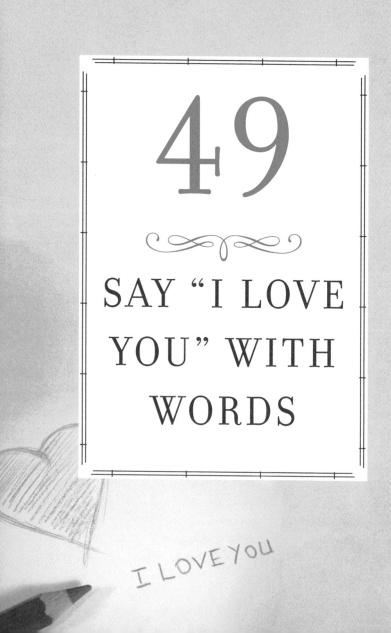

49

SAY "I LOVE YOU" WITH WORDS

I love you too."

What parent doesn't long to hear those words? Apparently, not many. Why else would there be so many wounded sons and daughters? Maybe you're an adult child who has longed your whole life to have Mom or Dad say, "I love you." You can keep your kids from experiencing that devastation by making certain your verbal expressions of affection include that three-word nugget of gold.

You might have grown up in a nondemonstrative family where love was not spoken, only acted on. In that kind of family, parents clean up after their kids, fill their cars with gas, return the library books, make the meals—the list goes on. They say they're doing this only because they care. Tangible deeds may underline love, but for some kids, such actions ring hollow without words to match.

Your relationship with your children colors their view of God. Parents stand in for the heavenly Father. Talk about filling huge shoes! Your using golden words expands your child's perspective of God's love for him or her. Are you standoffish or cold? Do you withhold needed nurturance? Your child will come to see God in that same light.

If your spouse never actually said, "I love you," you probably would have avoided saying, "I do." That simple proclamation keeps you on track when you wonder about your worth. Your children have that same need. Give them a home where love isn't silently acted out, but a place where they know for sure that they are loved in word as well as deed.

One more very tangible benefit: what you teach your children, they will almost certainly teach theirs. Imagine your grandchild one day nuzzling his or her head into your neck and whispering, "I love you" in your ear. It doesn't get better than that.

50

FIND A
CHURCH AND
STICK TO IT

Church families are as dysfunctional as any other. But they're also the place where you and your children learn to deal with problems, to grow, and to forgive. "Getting along" skills grow at church.

There are many different types of churchgoers. You have the only-on-Christmas-and-Easter crowd and the whenever-the-building's-open crew, and those who don't go anymore. The latter group sees church as a machine of abrasive parts and squeaking gears. But they may be missing the big picture. True church is a place of excitement where like minds gather for a greater purpose.

Choose a church home carefully—as carefully as you would choose a school district or a neighborhood. Read up on the denomination of the church you're considering to be sure that you can agree wholeheartedly with its beliefs. If you're still uncertain, don't hesitate to visit the pastor and ask questions. When you take your family for a visit, use your time to worship God. Once you step inside you have a choice: you can focus on incidentals and appearances, or you can get a feel for the pulse of friendliness flowing through.

Once you've found a church and feel settled, support your pastor and fellow believers. Otherwise you and your children will forever feel like outsiders and never learn the value of commitment.

Being faithful to your church is a way of showing unconditional love to flawed people. Show your kids it's okay to settle for the off-key earthly choir and a congregation full of people trying, but not quite there yet. Standing back in judgment isn't the answer—never has been. Only by joining in will you see discord disappear, joys heightened, and get a small sliver of your heavenly home.

51

RIDE OVER THE FALLS TOGETHER

The barrel reaches the edge of the splashing precipice. Thousands of gallons pour over, crashing down a slippery cliff. You and your barrel await the inevitable: the final tip toward destruction and the wettest, wildest ride of your life. Life can be like that ride over the falls.

If you've ever gone white-water rafting, you understand that it's all about expecting the unexpected. Sometimes things happen that are both unplanned and downright dangerous. Your raft hits a sharp rock and springs a leak. You're knocked unconscious after falling from the inflatable. Plummeting crashes happen.

Every family faces trauma. It's like traveling over a towering waterfall: down, down, down at breakneck speed. You aren't sure how you'll land and what condition you'll be in when you bob to the surface. One thing you can know—God is right there in your barrel with you.

Make a decision up front to stick together and trust God through thick and thin. At least that way you'll know that you can help your kids deal with what is going on around them, they can reach out for your help, and together you can depend on God's comfort and vast resources.

If you knew in advance the nature of the troubles ahead, you'd lose heart. That's why God shows us only the next necessary step on our journey. And He gives us courage only in the moment we most need it.

Working through problems with your family at your side provides the best and brightest chances for the future. No one has to battle life's storms alone. Regardless of the source of the white waters, your children should learn to reach out with two hands to grab God's and yours.

52

ROUND UP THE FAMILY FOR A REUNION

L ove 'em while you can. Your family is around for only a season, one that spins quickly past. A family reunion provides a
chance to build bonds before it's too late. You and your children see faces that once meant much and should mean more.

You'll also be able to connect with those whose time is short.
Such meeting and greeting means more than meals out. You and
your kids will touch and hug family history, ask questions that can
never be answered once the knowledge keepers leave—and stay up
way past bedtime.

When planning your reunion, look on the Internet for special
software that simplifies organization and planning. Include as many
far-flung cousins and in-laws as possible. You may find that the family tree has been engrafted with sturdy new branches. What an
opportunity to make new connections and reconnect with familiar
favorites. Plan a location where there's plenty to see and do. The
most difficult aspect may be finding food for varied palates. Don't go
too exotic unless everyone agrees in advance.

Listen together to tales from your youth. Laugh when someone
spills the beans about your own misadventures. Make sure you get
in your good-humored licks as well. It's good for your kids to see a
side of you they haven't known before.

Ask those who cannot attend to send photographs and return
the favor by taking enough pictures to send them copies. Your family circle will seem much more complete for the effort.

Your family heritage will stay strong only as long as the youngest
in the clan know the stories, both poignant and ridiculous. Children
should cherish chances to grow closer to their roots and stay con-
nected with family members who have become friends.

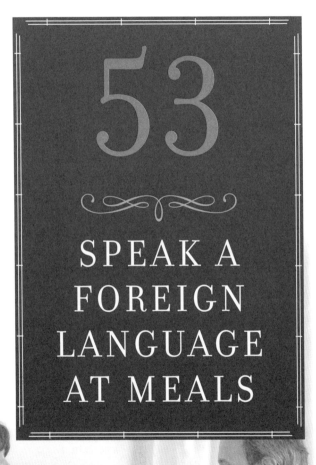

53

SPEAK A FOREIGN LANGUAGE AT MEALS

Chinese. Moroccan. Japanese. African. Italian. The world's your oyster. Pick your favorite ethnic restaurant and make a pact to enjoy an entire meal without resorting to English. The food will taste better, more authentic, when ordered in the native tongue. You and your children will have a great time trying to make yourselves understood to each other and the staff.

To get the most out of the experience, do your prep work. Find a language program that's family-friendly. Explore user comments online to pick one that will work for all ages. Then purchase it or check out a sampler at the library. Learn alongside your children but don't be discouraged if they pick up the language quicker than you do. Urge them to run on ahead. That way they'll be waiting for you when the time comes for your meal out.

If Mexican food is your choice, pick up some quick and easy Spanish vocabulary. Consider dressing the part. Elaborate costumes are not required, just something to enhance the cultural experience. Looking the part always helps your conversational bent.

Speak clearly and slowly and learn to say "Please repeat" in the native language. As you struggle for the right word, you'll realize the importance of building up your vocabulary. Be patient with yourself. When you're flustered, the pressure grows to lapse into English. You and your kids will get a tiny taste of the frustration a foreigner feels. Empathy expands as you stumble trying to speak your mind.

Communication means getting inside someone else's head. You and your children can accomplish this by wrapping your tongue around a new language and enjoying a delicious dinner in the process.

54

COLLABORATE ON A FAMILY MEMORY BOOK

Ever witness a car accident? Everyone differs on the details. You're sure you saw what you saw. But so's the next guy. And have you noticed how quickly memories fade? That's why collaborating with your kids on a family memory book makes sense. If only one person contributes all the anecdotes, you get a skewed picture. Honest impressions vary from person to person. Every addition broadens the perspective and gives a fuller picture.

Take your last vacation. You and your children probably had different ideas about fun. They wanted to hit the beach while you wanted a nap. The pictures show everyone grinning and giggling, but little likes and dislikes make us who we are. The ability to compromise and learn to enjoy more than we're used to shows true growth.

Perhaps one-half of the family enjoys adventure more than the other. Maybe Mom felt like leaning overboard as the sailboat bobbed along, while the kids climbed the rigging like pirates. There's a world of difference between how you felt seeing all those tombstone candles on your cake and the thrill your kids felt at decorating.

Logging the family memories proves to your kids that you can all have fun together, regardless of who's doing what, and looking through them will provide many hours of fun later on. You might even urge your youngsters to make their own smaller versions at the same time.

Scrapbooking is an entire industry now. Even if you aren't ready to launch into something that elaborate, you can find the supplies you need at any crafts store. Simple, simple, simple.

From making the memories together, recording them, creating a book to store them, and looking through them as the years go by, this project has limitless potential for fun, creativity, and bonding.

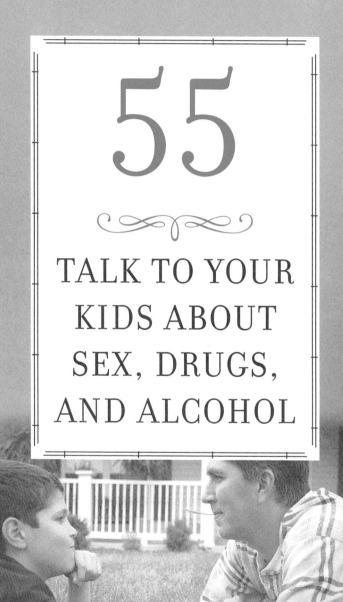

55

TALK TO YOUR KIDS ABOUT SEX, DRUGS, AND ALCOHOL

If you don't broach the "unbroachable," someone else will. The once-upon-a-time days of life without exposure to constant temptation are long gone. Virtually every television show, billboard, movie, ad, song, and video game raises once-taboo topics. You have to do some serious research to find truly family-friendly entertainment. For a lead-in to a discussion of sex, drugs, and alcohol, explore the resources on the Web. These are discussion starters only. Emphasize your personal values and beliefs when you dig into these issues.

Children now are as curious as you ever were—maybe more so. Strive to keep them innocent as long as possible but realize that they'll soon be old enough to talk about topics that never even crossed your mind at their age. The choice to avoid the problems must be made before the lure of addiction looms.

For example, your kids must decide to abstain from sex in advance of the opportunity. Similarly, drugs and alcohol should be avoided when someone pulls them out at a school dance or other seemingly innocuous affair. Research has found that kids whose parents talk to them about smoking are much less apt to try that first cigarette. Consistency counts. And so does banishing double standards.

Don't just discuss the negative stuff. Positive alternatives must be presented. Encourage their involvement in activities that keep their minds and bodies fully occupied. Challenge them. Let your kids end their day tired from learning, playing, or both. Boredom builds when they have too much time to kill.

Your example matters. Personal attitudes about healthy relationships and your conscious decision to avoid addicting behaviors can teach volumes. Help them see the joys of a full and fulfilled life without the unneeded dangerous additions.

56

※

RIDE A
ROLLER
COASTER
SIDE BY SIDE

R each for the sky! The next time you're at an amusement park and at least an hour past your last gooey snack, tackle one of the biggest attractions: the killer coaster. That'll coax gleeful screams from any rider. You and your kids will have a roaring good time as well. Explore local theme parks to find some challenging rides to add to your to-do list. There are probably at least a few close to where you live.

Waiting for your turn can seem to take forever. Ignore the grumbling. Try to convince the kids that the delay is part of the fun. Much as you'd like to, you can't run to the front of the line and hop on the next car. Roller coasters don't work that way. Neither does life. Talk together about patience: what it is, what it isn't, and why no one likes discussing it. Give examples of times when you couldn't have what you wanted right away. Tell how in retrospect you were glad God said no up front.

Once your turn arrives, hop aboard. Sit side by side so you can give or get comfort as needed. Feel the tingle of the slow climb— another chance for the excitement to build. You look at them; they look at you. Chills creep down your spine, then you feel the jolting pull, the stomach-clutching plunge, and fling your hands up. Laugh, scream, or holler, or do all three at once.

Trust the ride to stay on its track and enjoy the out-of-control sensation of being flung back and forth and whipped up and down. Let go together. Life imitates the roller coaster. No matter what highs and lows await, God sits right by your side.

57

READ A
CLASSIC
NOVEL
ALOUD

I magination flourishes when exercised. Regular read-aloud sessions with your kids will work wonders on their capacity to understand new situations. The flicker of video games, TV monitors, and computers goes to black when children start exploring the ghostly world of *A Christmas Carol*, survive the hardships of living in *Little House on the Prairie*, or travel heavenward in *Pilgrim's Progress*.

Explore the Internet for information on authors as well as online editions to preview. Once you've picked a classic, open to page one. That's the toughest part. Though daunting, it's the only way to conquer a journey of hundreds of pages. As you read on, your children will begin begging you for more.

Choose something with elements to entrance the youngest and enthrall the oldest—including you. Your kids will hear affection for the story in your cadence. Enthusiasm is catchy. Read during meals when the stragglers have swallowed their last few bites.

Watch your listeners. If their expressions say you need to clarify, stop the saga and explain. Encourage questions. Children can have amusing impressions of misunderstood words. Jot down humorous examples to enjoy later. If a book is well written and each chapter ends with cliff-hanging excitement, your children will long for the next installment. They'll want to see what happens, how the story grows. They may even applaud when you're through.

Whether reading Bible stories or the latest youth fiction bestseller, teach your kids to empathize with the intriguing characters. Learn from their mistakes, emulate their goodness. Your children will discover that's the point of all good literature: you see, you feel, you touch, and yet you have the chance to choose a better direction for yourself.

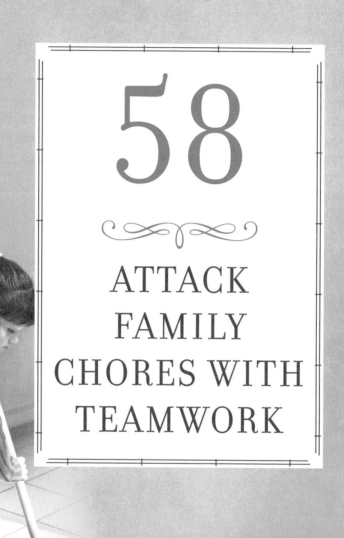

58

ATTACK
FAMILY
CHORES WITH
TEAMWORK

Mary Poppins somehow makes cleaning fun. Real-life cleanup can be pure drudgery. Part of the problem comes from psyching yourself into thinking the actual work will be too tough or take too long. Such fears exacerbate the problem and make you put off the inevitable, though tackling things early would have been a breeze.

Make the road between assignment and action short by leading the way and promising worthwhile rewards for success. Negative imprinting teaches kids to dread doing the hard stuff. The next time you have a major chore to do, talk to your kids about the family goals for the day. If they're on the same page, handling joint tasks can be downright fun.

Pitch in together whether it's garage-cleaning day or clean-up-the-yard weekend. Here's where Ms. Poppins might be onto something. Sing while you work and work as a team. Divide up the task into smaller steps: going through ten boxes of junk seems unbearable, but you could manage one a night. Think what treasures you and your children might find.

Another secret is to allot only a set time for your project. Twist the timer for an hour and work with all the energy you've got. You and your children know you're not stuck with an all-day struggle. Instead you can compete to beat the clock.

The family to-do list shrinks with total commitment. Plus your children learn to get tough jobs done without fussing or other typical time-wasting techniques. Work is a part of life. Don't leave your kids in the observer role when there's much to be done. Instill an ability to work both hard and smart. You'll give them a sense of accomplishment that reaps lifetime rewards.

59

❧

WATERPROOF
YOUR KIDS

B ackstroke, everyone! Though we all spent nine months in the watery womb, some kids still find swimming a terrifying prospect. But swimming safety is a must-have skill. Even if you live in the desert, waterproof your family.

Swim lessons are not always advisable. It depends on the ages, aptitude, and interests of your children. Not every child is ready to start training in the pool. Explore this topic further online or at your local library. When they are ready, sign them up for class at your local Y or public park swimming program. Teaching them yourself is an option, but many find their children listen better to a trained instructor.

First, your kids need to learn to get their faces wet and blow bubbles. Teach this in the tub. Get a few Ping-Pong balls and have your little ones blow them across the water.

Acquaint younger children with the pool when they're ready. Often they need to get used to the idea. Help them step off the edge and into the wet. When they're ready, let them jump in. A hula hoop target can entice them.

Learning to float is a crucial skill. Show them how to simply lie over the top of the water. Nervous children curl up into balls and sink. Teach them to relax and flatten out. Once that's mastered they need to get comfortable holding their breath and ducking under the water. Encourage them as they're ready but don't push too far or too fast.

Soon your kids will be ready to propel themselves along and you'll have the swiftest swimmers in the fish school. Swimming is a healthy activity you can enjoy together. They'll love it, and you'll rest easier knowing your children won't sink.

60

LIE BACK ON
THE GRASS
AND EXAMINE
THE CLOUDS

Few pleasures match stretching out on a blanket to watch the clouds go by. What could be more relaxing?

Go online or visit your library to learn a bit more about the type of clouds you and your kids will see and what they mean for the upcoming weather. It's nice to know when a downpour is imminent.

You'll be amazed at the pictures forming above you. Volcanoes bubble over, flop-eared bunnies pose, or maybe that's the face of the president of the United States or Mr. Potato Head! There are no wrong answers. Take turns pointing out what you see. Keep a sketch pad on hand to copy some of the craziest shapes.

You and your kids might want to take a CD player outside to enjoy the clouds with beautiful background accompaniment. See who can find the most pictures. Let everyone share what he or she sees. Feel free to disagree on what's what and even which side is up! The fact that the clouds are constantly changing adds to the challenge. You may all agree that you've spotted Winnie-the-Pooh in the puffy white cloud above but then sigh as he turns into a pot of honey.

Trying to see someone else's pictures can be challenging, but your children will pick up a gentle life lesson. Things that seem so clear and obvious to them may not even be recognizable to someone else.

When you take the time to explain the gaping mouth, big pointy ears, or floppy feet, suddenly the picture takes shape, has meaning. Clearly, it's a clown. Finally, you all agree. Your kids will learn that not all people see things their way or even the same way. But observing through each other's eyes improves everyone's vision.

61

FIND A JOKE
AND TELL IT
UNTIL YOUR
KIDS BEG YOU
TO STOP

K nock-knock. Who's there?
    Canoe. Canoe who?
    Canoe lend me some more money?

Okay, so maybe that hits a little too close to home for some parents. But it's still kind of funny. For collections of similar knock-knock classics, check out your local library.

Joke telling is an art. Improve your audience approval rating by shaping the outlines of the joke in your mind before opening your mouth. Whatever you do, have the punch line down cold before diving in. It can be hilarious watching someone murder a joke, but it's not quite the same when you're the hapless performer.

For a comic, timing is everything. Even deciding when to tell your joke matters. Wow them when they least expect it and when the mood is right. Never prep your kids with promises of perfection. Let your storytelling and quality material speak for itself. Or not.

When you're setting up your joke, include all the relevant details. Practice, practice, practice that punch line until you've got it letter-perfect. Remember: no pausing and no "wait-a-minute" excuses. Just say your piece, smile, and stand back for the laughter—or rotten fruit. Whenever you hear a clean classic, jot down the details so you can share it with your kids. Start a collection of your personal best. And once you stumble upon a winner, stand ready to tell it at the slightest provocation.

Levity is a gift—one you have the power to give your children. Besides, won't it be fun to hear them complain to their siblings long into adulthood, "Hey, do you remember that terrible joke Dad used to tell us about the . . .?" Groans and moans. "Oh no, please—not that one!"

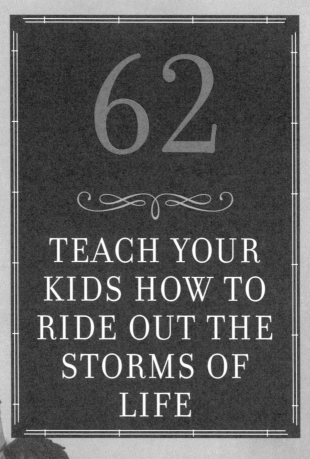

62

TEACH YOUR
KIDS HOW TO
RIDE OUT THE
STORMS OF
LIFE

It's all good." You've seen that message on cards, in frames, maybe even on a cross-stitch sampler. The scriptural source for the message talks of God working out everything for our good (Rom. 8:28). When your family trembles through trauma, you can't help wondering how it is for the best. Reaching that peaceful plateau can seem to take forever.

Another approach is the "This too shall pass" mentality. But that makes you feel as if you're doing something wrong and must wait for good luck to return. A time will come to tell your kids that life is tough. Sometimes you won't even be in the boat when the ocean starts churning. You'll barely be treading water.

When inevitable difficulties occur, your response will light the way for your kids. Do you curse God and blame Him for the mistakes you made? Or do you take a deeper look at the situation and learn from failed opportunity? Despite the pain, reason can reign. With practice you can weed out patterns that drive you and your children into the ruts of life—though that doesn't mean you'll avoid all the bumps in the road.

God stands alongside you. You can and will get through sickness, job loss, sadness, and pain. Though climbing that difficult hill hurts, you can outlast the bruising storm.

In life's ebb and flow, allow your children to see both good and bad. Don't focus on the latter or ignore the former. Our roughest moments are less so because of God's presence. Teach your children this truth and give them a lifeline of hope, something secure to hang onto when you are no longer there to help them through difficult waters.

63

STAGE A CONTROLLED FOOD FIGHT

G o ahead—play with your food. This may be your first foray or you could come from a long line of grub slingers. Your children won't believe their luck at experiencing a food fight in the privacy of their own backyard.

Here's a parentally sanctioned opportunity to forget good manners, get silly, and have an ooey-gooey experience like no other.

First, plan this for a warm spell so you can use the hose for cleanup. Keep the mushy memory alive by designating a photographer. Then set the ground rules. Use only squishy, wet, and sticky stuff. No tossing ham bones or anything that could really hurt or poke out an eye. Choose sides, put up opposing picnic tables, put on swimsuits or play clothes, and have a snowball fight with food. Use soft fresh fruit like bananas, and maybe some canned peaches, apricots, and pineapples—without the cans, of course. Get a bunch of cheap pie tins and fill them with whipped cream. Each team member gets a store of them for the finale.

After you draw the battle lines, declare war! Toss the goo, heave those creamy "pies," and laugh until you can't stand it. Feel the thrill of a well-placed splat. When someone smears a teammate, get them back. Splish-splash, squish, mash.

You'll have a disaster area when you're done. Gather up the remnants to feed the birds, squirrels, or other lucky neighborhood critters.

Your food fight will give your children a taste for battle. They'll see that little squabbles can become big ones as revenge roars into motion. One person hits another, who hits back—and so it goes. Though your family food fight fun may cause an enormous mess, no lasting harm is done. Help your kids see that harsh words hurt far more than cream pies.

64

PILE UP THE PILLOWS, DIM THE LIGHTS, AND WATCH A MOVIE

Camaraderie: it holds armies, companies, and families together. The next time your stress level shoots off the scale, take a break. Slip into pj's, set out a few quick snacks, grab pillows and blankets, and camp out around the TV. Pull out a sofa sleeper and stretch out to watch with the kids. Keep the film light, the lights low, and the mood upbeat. Outlaw all serious thoughts. Banish them as you spend time with your children.

As you sit together in the dark, treasure the moment. Enjoy the silliness both on- and offscreen. Don't fuss over shopping or to-do lists or put-off chores. Your responsibilities are officially on hold. Slip into the moment and forget tomorrow's worries. Those troubles will still be there when you're ready to face them again.

Time spent with your children often comes while too many pots sit simmering in the background, so they don't get your full attention. Take this cool respite to rest, turn off the world, and comfort yourselves with snuggles and closeness all around.

Your children will love it and you will too. Note carefully how your kids forget homework, bikes in the driveway, the lawn they promised to mow last weekend. They're fully engaged, fully into the fun. Learn from their example.

Together you'll see the value of living in and for the moment once in a while. It's not a sin. The Bible mandates that we live worry-free. What's the point of fussing over the future when only God holds that key? During those brief couple of hours of "lights out," get over the humdrum, the hovering schedule, and focus on the fun and family.

65

PLAN A "TOUR DE NEIGHBORHOOD" BIKE RACE

D o you even know the names of the thousands of souls who are living nearby? Did you move in, unpack, and let the years pass before sharing more than a perfunctory hello? You're busy, they're busy, but that's no excuse. You and your children can pull hearts and homes together by staging a Tour de Neighborhood for all comers.

Invite anyone with a bike, scooter, roller skates, or wheelchair to participate. Closeness is the goal, not competitiveness. The slower you go, the more opportunity you'll have to get to know people. First, go door-to-door with invitations; pass out the "tour" map. Keep it simple—maybe a scenic trip to a nearby park. Limit the distance traveled for those who might be a bit out of shape. Build bonds but avoid having anyone pass out from the effort.

En route, snap pictures to share later. End the event with everyone bringing a favorite topping for an ice-cream social at your house. All you have to do is buy a couple tubs of vanilla, put out plastic bowls and spoons, and scoop until you can't scoop anymore.

Your children will see that being neighborly is normal, that hospitality is a joy. That's important in a world where technology affords us the opportunity to become more and more self-sufficient—and isolated. Schedules keep us sitting in the minivan rather than sitting on the porch. Our back fences, once a social gathering place, have been replaced by six-foot-tall privacy fences. It's now possible to live within a few feet of your neighbors and never learn their names.

Kids need to see and appreciate the power of community, to draw from the give-and-take neighbors have to offer. Your tour will help you and your kids make valuable connections.

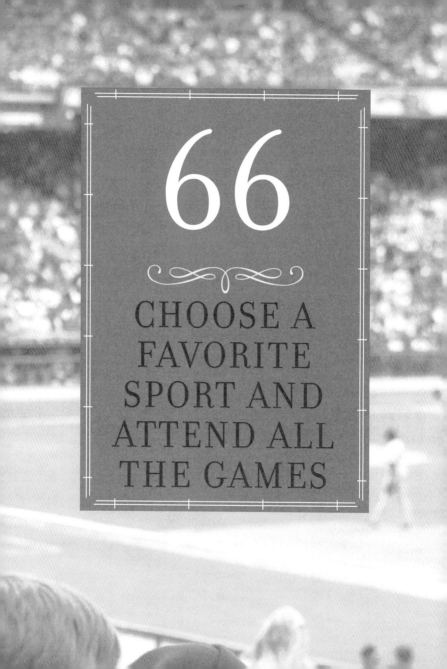

66

CHOOSE A
FAVORITE
SPORT AND
ATTEND ALL
THE GAMES

Commitment. It's the essence of a solid marriage, the core of our relationship with God, and the reason we love our kids even when they drive us crazy. Pick a favorite sport and team and stick with 'em no matter which way the wind blows. Faithfully show up and cheer, and mean what you scream! You and your crew will become the working definition of die-hard fans.

If you can't afford the fees involved with a professional sporting activity, get behind your church or work league. Pick an underdog bowling team. Doesn't matter. Just find a group of players and support them with your time and attention. Have your children jot down the names of the team members. Meet them at breaks and offer the occasional pat on the back or "Attaboy!"

It's always much more fun if everyone knows the rules of the sport you plan to follow. That doesn't need to be a long process. Study them together and quiz each other on the particulars.

There's a chance that your team will play so horribly that you'll want to cringe. Buck up. They're still yours. Stand and shout: "Let's go, guys! You can do it!" Keep supporting them no matter how they're performing.

Not only will your kids pick up a pointer or two about a favorite activity, they'll see the importance of sticking with someone—not because the person is the best, the fastest, or the most beautiful—but simply because your kids said they would.

That's like playing on God's heavenly league. We don't deserve a slot on the starting lineup, but He pulled a few strings. And win or lose, He's always there cheering us on.

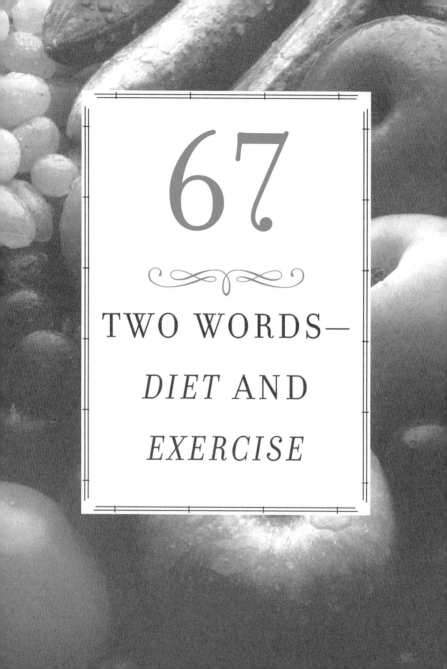

67

TWO WORDS—

DIET AND

EXERCISE

Ever hope there's more to you than what you eat—especially when you review a week's worth of junk you've gobbled? Maybe the scale says it's time for a few more salads and fewer desserts. Could be your children are facing the battle of the bulge too.

If so, make a family commitment to adopt healthier way of eating. It's easy to fall into patterns of snacking while watching TV, eating too late, or even eating what upsets your stomach. Bad habits can be broken and bent into better directions. If your children are already fitting a bit too snugly into the family mold, take immediate steps.

The "die" word comes first. Your "die"-t doesn't have to be terrible, but it must include balanced, calorie-conscious meals. Snacks and sweets, especially soft drinks and juices, must be curtailed. Cut down the number of times you go out. Once your family gets a taste of the healthful alternatives, they won't want to go back.

Part two is exercise. Start a simple program incorporating stretches and walking. As you become more accustomed to the program, add in some push-ups, sit-ups, and easy free weights to build up the arms and upper body. Take advantage of exercise programs on television.

Some kids take naturally to healthy living. It will be more of a challenge for some to get on track. Be persistent. With time, even the most reluctant will grow to like the benefits of living a healthier life.

When you help your kids join good eating with healthy exercise patterns, you increase the likelihood of their having longer, happier lives. And you help them avoid mistakes you've made. Look at your watch. Is it almost time to eat? Make some changes now, before you set the table.

68

❧

WALK IN
THE RAIN
WITH ONE
UMBRELLA

There's nothing like a spring shower. The next time a gentle rain impinges on plans, make the best of it. Invite the whole crew to huddle under the brim of one big umbrella and take a walk. As long as you're not out in a hurricane or lightning, you'll all be able to catch a little protection from the sprinkles. More than that, you'll have fun getting wet and standing close to those you love.

Walk slowly. Notice how beautiful the washed world looks. Street signs shimmer, passing cars glimmer. Everything is clean. Control yourself or you may start "singin' in the rain." (Although that might be fun, especially if you enjoy mortifying your children!)

While rain-walking you'll see things you've never noticed from a car or city bus: Water washing in rivulets from downspouts. Flowers drooped with moisture. Cats and dogs shaking off droplets. You gain a whole different perspective when you're out in the weather rather than closed in at home.

Enjoy the closeness with your kids. Take turns holding the umbrella. The younger ones may have to stretch their arms and stand on tippy-toe and the taller ones might need to crouch. When you're under an umbrella together you need to give a little, share a little. You'll learn about teamwork and watching out for the other guy or gal's comfort.

You'll also discover that God's rain does indeed fall on all of us. You won't see one house set apart, standing high and dry in the blazing sun. When it rains, everyone gets wet. Likewise, God's love is a gift of grace that pours down on all of us with plenty to spare.

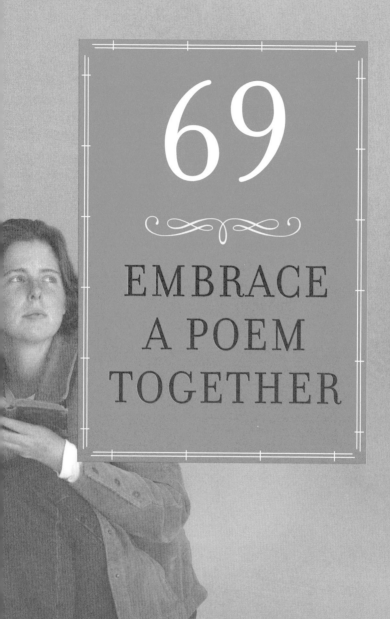

69

❧

EMBRACE
A POEM
TOGETHER

D own with poetry!" some say. Why all the negative attitudes toward poems? Maybe you got a bad taste in your mouth from an anxious teacher who kept the thrill and meaning of a sonnet at arm's length. Good poetry is accessible—or should be. Every song you love, greeting card that makes you giggle, and even passages from your favorite novelists use poetic language. Rhyming is irrelevant.

Try a family poetry evening. Pick a poem your whole family will enjoy. Perhaps an A.A. Milne classic about Winnie-the-Pooh, or something from Shel Silverstein. Skip the reruns and read aloud. Whatever you do, don't merely say the words; think about them first. Get into the meaning behind the phrases to discover the poet's intent. Use your emotions and speak as loudly, quietly, or plainly as needed to make the poem come alive.

Consider having everyone pick a short ditty to commit to memory. (Of course, you will almost certainly have to help out with the selections.) Not only will your kids be challenged, but they will sharpen a much-neglected faculty. Some things, like multiplication tables, must be learned by heart. This exercise shows them they can succeed.

When everyone has his or her poem firmly implanted, have a special evening performance. Keep it low-key. You'll be as nervous and excited as the rest of the crew. Both hearer and speaker gain new understanding as poetic images sparkle.

Poetry refuses to let us gloss over deep meanings. It forces us to think and gives us time to ponder both joy and pain. Your child's life is a poem written by God. Help your offspring discover the beauty of the Creator written on the soul.

70

TEACH YOUR KIDS TO "BE QUIET AND LISTEN"

Rudeness happens. Sometimes shock and shame rock us as we watch kids talk, talk, talk but ignore what's being said. Blame it on the culture, blame it on yourself, but take steps to prevent that blight from further smearing your family name.

Parents and children are not created equal. We're not on par even if we like to pretend that's the case. When you're only pals and not parents, you upset a delicate balance that God set in place. If you've fallen into such permissive patterns, you can probably testify to its ineffectiveness and your frustration.

At times you have things to say that your children must hear even if they'd rather not. This is not license to filibuster or browbeat, but permission for you to take the floor and hold it. You've also got a wealth of experiences that could prevent pain. That's why, in the course of familial events, it may become necessary for you to gently but firmly say, "Be quiet and listen."

This becomes necessary when the buzzing is so loud and the arguments so insidious that communication crumbles. Or worse, it becomes a blocked one-way street. God wants parents to assert their rightful role and stop playing doormat to demanding, undisciplined children.

When they leave home, your kids will undoubtedly be confronted with authority in the form of a professor or employer. They will be miles ahead if they have learned to treat such people with respect and listen quietly when they speak.

So, when the moment comes—and you'll know when it does—put your foot down and grab the attention you deserve. Make your pitch with sincerity. Assure them they'll have plenty of time afterwards for questions and discussion. Such honesty sets a pattern for solidifying faltering relationships and bolstering strong ones.

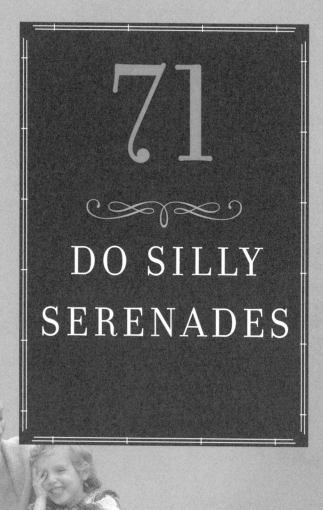

71

DO SILLY
SERENADES

E ver get a singing telegram? It's payback time. The tradition of serenading your beloved has a long history. Even the most musically challenged have participated with pride. Years ago, a young man would sing loudly to his lady love as she swooned from a second-story dormitory window. Such spontaneity makes serenades special—or at least memorable.

You sing your child to sleep as you rock her small form. Look that little one in the eye until she nods off. Stare at her beautiful features. You might want to make the lyrics personal by inserting your child's name where appropriate. Children love to be singled out. Youngsters delight in having their siblings' names woven into the verses too.

Unfortunately, that gentle interest in lullaby time won't last as children reach the in-between years. They'll develop mixed emotions about your singing, even if you're belting out a tune in their honor. They abhor an audience at that age. If you must croon, keep it low-key and on key. Maybe you'll get special dispensation to solo on a birthday, but don't hold your breath. Warn sleepyheads that they're fair game for a rousing get-out-of-bed ditty if the alarm is ignored.

During the teen years, you may need to serenade your young adult with a heartsong accompanied by a voice of silence. Unless immune to mortification, your teenager won't thank you for showing up at the pizza parlor or school game to sing. He'll thank you if you don't! Fortunately this awkward stage passes in a few years.

One day your attempts at song may be welcomed at graduation, on your son or daughter's wedding day, or at the birth of your grandchild. When the time comes, hold your kids close and quietly sing, "Jesus Loves You." They'll remember.

72

TAKE A NIGHTTIME STROLL THROUGH THE GALAXY

Y ou're no accident—and neither are your children. The truth of this statement blazes in the night sky. Those stars above fling light outward in an ever-expanding universe. That means, of course, that in the beginning our world had a launching point. And Someone hit the "start" button.

He was there at the dawn of time and awaits our arrival at the finish line, a truth visible in the stars. Remind your children that their planet earth rests securely in God's strong hands.

Look up tonight. Can your kids find the North Star, Ursa Major, or even Ursa Minor? If not, it may be time to get to know your home galaxy. These unique patterns helped guide sailors around the globe and will point your family to the Creator. With a little effort you can prepare a personal star tour for them.

Before you begin, consult your library or the Internet. With some tools, you'll be able to identify some of the most familiar stellar formations. Reflect aloud on the fact that God placed those stars in the sky. Think of it! He knew that one day you and your kids would be looking up together and that they would remind you of Him.

Young men and women dream of star-soaring. Astronauts have tripped along on the moon, and a Mars launch may be just years away. Time will tell. Yet no matter how far we travel, we can't escape God's watchful eye. He sees us through the brightest light and darkest night. Share that truth with your children.

God made all, knows all. He cares for your children enough to create the perfect balance of sun, stars, and planets. Without question, our world was intentionally, intelligently planned. So were they.

73

REMIND YOUR
KIDS THAT
CLEANLINESS IS
NEXT TO
GODLINESS

Ever open the door of a child's room and feel as if the mess might jump out and grab you? Contrary to most parents' expectations, kids are—with a few notable exceptions—not naturally neat. In fact, most are freakishly not neat!

It's never too early to insist on simple rules that can affect health: washing hands before meals, brushing and flossing teeth, clipping fingernails. When it comes to these things, early expectations clearly presented will prevent problems later.

The same is true of establishing a sense of orderliness. If you want your kids to make their beds, instill that habit as soon as your child can pull up the sheets by himself. (Be sure you're making yours as well.) Same goes for picking up clothes and putting away toys. With repetition these basic life skills become second nature. But you'll have to keep after the kids until these skills become engrained. A checklist taped to a bathroom mirror works wonders, especially if privileges are revoked when reminders are ignored.

Cleanliness reflects inner pride. Your child's self-worth shows in clothing choices and hair decisions. Sometimes there's no nefarious subplot, no boiling turmoil. Kids simply follow trends. However, if you see bizarre twists in appearance grow into disrespect for the family, tap into a professional's expertise.

Regular showers, clean face and hair, and neat rooms are requirements of polite society—and should be established habits well before your child leaves home. Your kids need to see that appearances matter—to prospective employers, roommates, potential spouses. They tell the world how a person views himself. Teach your kids the importance of making a lasting but not lingering impression.

74

<hr>

TEACH YOUR KIDS GOOD STUDY TECHNIQUES

Good study habits set your child up for scholarly success. Distraction-free time for schoolwork opens the door wider. You or your spouse may have graduated from the put-it-off-until-midnight school of academic preparation. Let that tradition die with you. Make the necessary sacrifices to allow your kids the chance to shine.

Come clean with your kids. Talk to your children about mistakes you made and how you wish you'd had a specific time and place to prepare assignments. Admit your shortcomings, but go a step farther and point out their immense potential.

Results improve when you take a disciplined approach to test taking or paper writing. Working step by step allows regular reinforcement plus the advantage of avoiding overload. Encourage your kids to write down their goals and date items when crossed off their list. Get them to see the long view. Studying hard now opens up opportunities for the future: maybe a good job, professional fulfillment, or the funds needed to support a family. Consistently good attitudes reap rewards later.

All work can be tiring, and mental gymnastics can be especially exhausting. Make sure your kids take breaks and have snacks available to recharge their energy. Teach them that prayer can also help them to focus on the work at hand even as it nourishes the soul. The reward of a few minutes of fun after a rigorous study session motivates the continuing study cycle.

Show your children the value in learning for learning's sake. Nothing's more satisfying. Even if everyone else "gets it" first, that's OK. These things even out over time, as you know from experience. True growth means grasping challenging concepts for yourself. Urge them to reach out and do that.

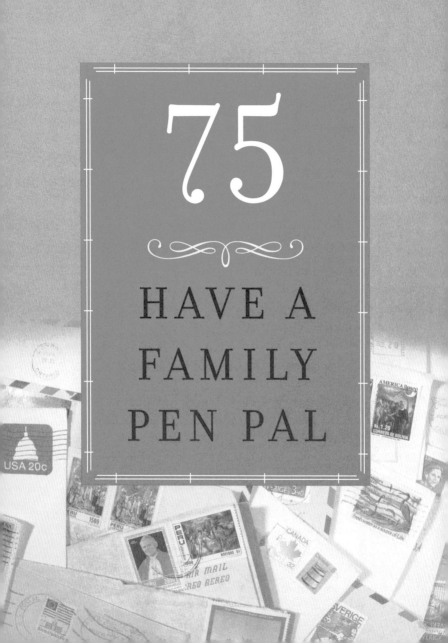

75

HAVE A
FAMILY
PEN PAL

Children and prisoners like it; so do military women and men, and your maiden aunt: snail mail. In this e-mail age of instant messaging and quick, random communication, people forget how much a letter can mean, especially to the lonely.

A family pen pal allows your kids to make a new friend and discover ways to uplift through the cherished but oft overlooked medium of correspondence. Look at your own circle of acquaintances and select a person who would enjoy hearing the latest buzz from your crew. Consider nominating someone who lives alone or far from home.

Another option is writing to a child in a third-world country via a relief organization. Many organizations want donors to send personal correspondence to sponsored children. Your kids will love getting pictures from the other side of the world and hearing about the life of a person whose reality is very different from their own.

Letter writing can be a slow, thoughtful process. That's as it should be. Take your time to carefully choose your phrases, feel for the right words. To succeed as a correspondent, you and your children must open your hearts. Your family pen pal teaches your children that letters can bring hope to both writer and recipient.

Truth resonates in a two-way discussion. The lag in the back-and-forth response time allows anticipation to build. Your kids will become accustomed to waiting for the daily delivery.

As you create your family letter, remind your young writers about a remarkable letter of love penned just for them: the Bible. They can read it anytime, no stamps or waiting required.

76

MAKE
PERSONAL
TRIUMPHS
A FAMILY
AFFAIR

Light shouldn't be trapped under a bushel barrel. Good news shouldn't be wasted either. Notice when something big happens to your kids. Trumpet your child's accomplishments and celebrate them together—even if you have to look closely to see them.

Different children have different capabilities. Honest efforts from whiz kids *and* slow learners deserve recognition and reward. Never favor one child because he tests well. Focus on accomplishment rather than sheer potential. Be willing to see beyond tight smiles to the struggles beneath the mask. What came easy for you might be a brain bender for them. A C+ in a tough class deserves to be heralded every bit as much as an A in an easy one—probably more so.

Successes large or small should be announced at family meals and in year-end newsletters. Think of unique ways to say "Congratulations"—maybe a special meal out or an elaborate Chinese dinner brought in. If your children enjoy books or clothes, find gift certificates that they can use as they please. They'll appreciate the bonus and you'll love seeing what happens when positive efforts are reinforced.

When you make a point of getting the whole family into the act, your children realize you're proud enough to burst. Everyone relishes the well-deserved limelight. Kids need to cheer for each other as well. It teaches them how to enjoy someone else's being center stage—an important life skill.

Individual accomplishments grow when sprinkled with encouragement. Show how pleased you are when your child triumphs. Let your kids know that God is smiling on them too! Make sure your whole family shares in the excitement. They'll be more inclined to cheer knowing their turn will come.

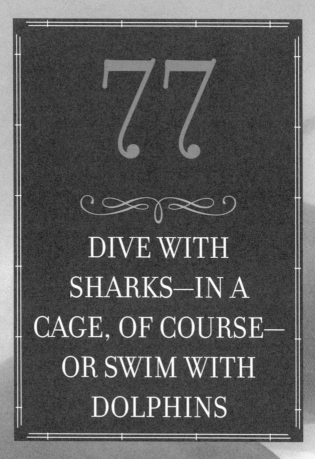

77

DIVE WITH SHARKS—IN A CAGE, OF COURSE— OR SWIM WITH DOLPHINS

S harks and dolphins mesmerize fans with their fins. Their flowing forms challenge our assumptions about control. Underwater animals rule a liquid domain much different from our own. We must either invade their world or bring them into an aquarium to see firsthand their mystery and majesty.

For an adventure of mammoth proportions, take your children to Tampa, Florida, and give them a chance to swim with the sharks. The experience is for divers with wetsuits so you'll need to plan ahead. Once there, you'll wait safely behind bars in a shark cage. Then you can watch as the amazing creatures come in nose-to-nose for a closer look. If sharks are a bit much for the kids, you can turn your attention to dolphins, which are every bit as intriguing as sharks. Known for their friendliness, they're often thought of as water-bound pets. In the wild they leap, play, and curiously probe your boat.

Sharks and dolphins bring beauty and balance to the undersea world. Both must eat to live, both bear young, and both possess God-given power and intelligence. Over the years they've earned very different reputations: one as a cold-blooded killer and the other as man's water buddy.

As you and your kids study these animals, you'll have the chance to cast your own vote. But withhold judgment until that up-close-and-personal encounter. You might be surprised at which creature comes in first as the family favorite.

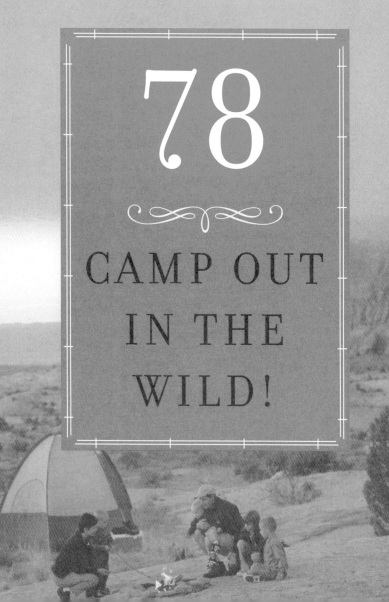

78

CAMP OUT
IN THE
WILD!

Head for the hills. Depending on your family's adventure quotient, camping out may mean lodging with rows of other RV-ers. Or you may picture a perfectly pitched tent as you forage for supper. Some sleep in the safety and comfort of a car. Different families have different ideals.

Work with whatever your family calls "wild." You might start by exploring online for a list of national parks. Take along the practical necessities of fresh water, toilet facilities, good food, medical supplies for scrapes, bee stings, and poison ivy itching, and a camera, but be sure to avoid overpacking. The less you take in, the less you'll have to haul out . . . and the less you'll strain your back.

Let God's natural backdrop provide the entertainment. Ban all electronics. Instead spend the evening talking, listening to the crickets, and shivering to a coyote's howl. For your first camping foray, keep the trip short and hopefully sweet. You don't want your kids begging to go home but pleading to stay. That's the mark of success.

Your senses will blossom in the wild of God's creation. You and your children will hear rustling and scraping, wiggling and sniffing. Those mystery creatures are hungry animals and you're in their territory. Carefully store food in clean, odor-proof bins and tie other edibles high above the site to avoid tempting unwelcome eaters.

Camping in the wild always surprises—often in a good way. Wieners on a stick become luxury dining as you and your kids learn to appreciate small pleasures. The noisy night in the wild becomes quite attractive when compared to the hustle and bustle of busy living. Relaxation and peace are civilized pursuits after all. Savor this respite and plan to return with your family as soon as possible.

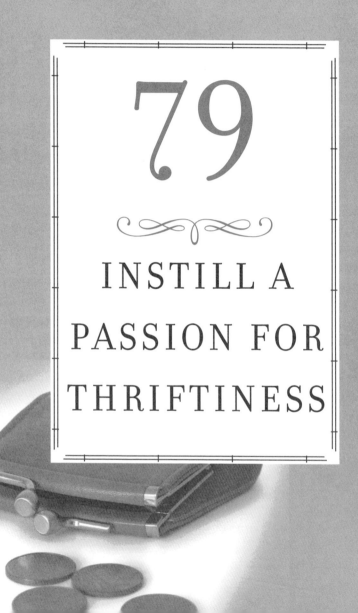

79

INSTILL A PASSION FOR PASSION FOR THRIFTINESS

W hat do your kids want? Wish lists expand as product availability grows. The more there is, the more they "need." The bigger the item, the better. Kids feel constricted to the no-fun zone when they lack the trendiest toys. They could do so much more if they only had the money. Maybe you know the feeling.

The good old days of a continually soaring economy have been replaced by financial ups and downs. As companies downsize, families are forced to adjust expectations. Help your kids see that putting food on the table and living in a warm home are not rights, but privileges. Talk about those who have far less than they do. Remind them that the brand-new vehicles and latest technological gadgets will have to wait.

Thriftiness goes against the flow, and you can't convincingly make the case if you're pushing your credit to the limits. The "let's make do" message rings false if you're grabbing all you can with both hands. Teach your children that satisfaction exists apart from possessions and plans for the future. Credit companies highlight what you'll be getting, not what you'll owe.

Graphically show your children the high cost of buying with borrowed money. At the mall, pick up the shoes they've been begging for. Offer to lend them money to buy them. But explain that you'll charge interest, which means they'll pay double or triple for the same pair of sneakers. Isn't it better to save for what you want rather than buying before you can afford to?

Live happily on less than you earn and you'll understand contentment. Cash never brings joy, but being satisfied with God's good gifts does. Teach your kids that it's not only possible but preferable to stretch money until it snaps—and then some.

80

DIG FOR CLAMS
AND STEAM
THEM ON THE
BEACH

Clammers unite! How often do you have the chance to hunt for your dinner while watching the Maker's hands spin the crashing surf? You can enjoy a delicacy: the sweetest, most tender clams you've ever had. And you can give your children a taste for what's involved in finding and preparing their own meal courtesy of God's creation.

First, find a beach. Whether hailing from the Atlantic or Pacific side, you'll be able to capture clams. Check local weather conditions and locate a promising shore. Clams are scooped from the moist sand at low tide and ready and waiting year round. Depending on the variety, your clams may be hard- or soft-shelled. You and your kids will find them chewy and tasty. To steam them, fill a pot with about one to two inches of boiling water, then cover and steam the clams over an open fire until they pop open—at least six minutes to assure thorough heating. Throw away unopened clams and enjoy the rest with sautéed garlic and onions. Add a bowl of macaroni and cheese and some fresh fruit and your oceanside meal is complete. You'll fall in love with the flavor.

Too often we simply order a meal or throw something in a microwave. Rarely do we have to enter into the behind-the-scenes prep work of bringing food from prey to plate. We appease our appetites without trouble or sacrifice.

Clam digging gives your gang a chance to reconnect with each other and have some wet, sandy fun. Plus they see for themselves that there's work involved in putting daily bread (and clams) on the table. Hunting for hidden clams works up an appetite. In an age of all-too-available, all-you-can-eat buffets, you'd do well to teach your kids to catch their own food for a change.

81

❧

FOSTER
FAMILY
FRIENDSHIPS

Best friends: we all long for them, cling to them, and feel devastated when they move away. That's as it should be. Truth is, though, the best friends your kids could ever hope for live right under your roof. Despite popular mythology to the contrary, siblings were meant to be buddies. Ignore the psychobabble about rivalry and birth order. If you choose to, you can foster a love and respect between your kids that will last longer than you do. Imagine siblings who care enough to comfort each other when you're gone.

To accomplish this, forget about favorites. The Bible is replete with tales of parents picking out a "best kid" and pouring on the goodies. Remember Joseph and his amazing, multicolored coat? The other brothers were fit to be tied at the gift. So they got revenge by tying Joseph up and selling him as a slave. Sadly, hatred of one child for another is common and usually results from a parent doting on Child A while ignoring Child B.

Children understand the pecking order. They pick up on what's happening. If you're not careful, they begin questioning your fairness. Parents who prefer one child over another make a monstrous mistake. Why say sweet Susie is smarter, nicer, or a better athlete than little Johnny? Such talk destroys any chance for friendship between your kids. It can also instill sturdy superiority and inferiority complexes. Some kids figure they don't have to work hard and others wonder "What's the use?"

Nurture your children equally and they'll have a better chance of getting along. They'll learn that they differ in gifts and strengths. By encouraging them to be friends, they lean on each other in their weak areas. Brothers and sisters can also be friends who stay close forever.

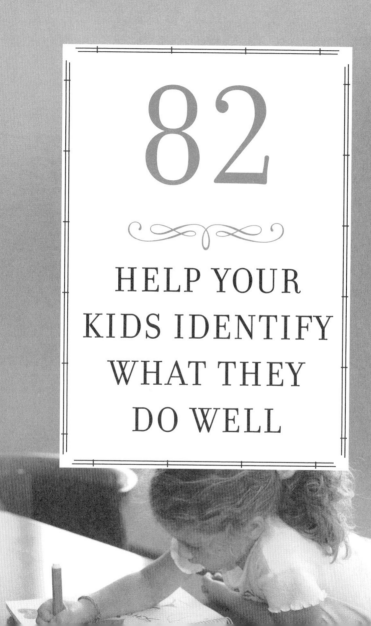

82

HELP YOUR KIDS IDENTIFY WHAT THEY DO WELL

I t might be right before their eyes—and yet invisible to them. That's one reason your children need you to help them see their God-given abilities. Forget fears of sounding prideful. Give encouraging praise when and where it's due. You're in the best position to see their uniqueness.

Every child needs something that makes him feel stand out special. What that personal gift might be varies. Even within a family, kids will differ in what they can and like to do. One may enjoy helping the handicapped or solving tangled problems that others can't deal with. Maybe they're great at something the world fails to recognize with gold medals. Wonderful—we need a whole lot more just like them.

Sometimes the daily grind wears you down. You long for encouragement yourself but come up empty. That's no excuse. You still need to help your children see the good within. Pointing out positives about their personalities and abilities accomplishes that.

Go one step farther and find out what skills they want or would like to strengthen. Then teach them if you can or encourage them to gain the knowledge in an after-school class. With the plethora of online courses and books, your child should be able to learn just about anything.

Most of all, ask God to give you insights into His gifts in your children's lives. Then ask Him how best to help draw those out.

Make your children's well-being a top priority. Help them grow as people. Realize their self-sufficiency and personal worth are guided by how they value themselves. That's typically a function of their talents. Each one has special skills stitched in by the Creator, but more important, they are His children.

83

SCHOOL YOUR
KIDS IN WAYS
TO MANAGE
CONFLICT

U ntil we're all perfect and lined up to sing in God's choir, conflict will happen. Your kids' angelic demeanor slips into something else right before your eyes and tempers flare.

Like all children of Adam and Eve, we're rule-breakers at heart. We make mistake after mistake. How we handle these situations is the real test. When your children challenge your resolve, you must stay strong for their sake and yours. Conflict arises most often from a failure to address problems diplomatically, to handle small concerns before they fester.

You and your kids will inevitably struggle for control. Your children will also have squabbles with siblings, clashes with classmates, and assorted run-ins with the rest of civilization. How they deal with difficulties, however, begins and ends with you.

Teach them to pause and take a breath. The worst possible course is the leap from imagined injury to riled response—zero to outraged in less than sixty seconds.

Far better to step back and engage the brain before opening the mouth. This delay mechanism prevents a torrent of words you or they will want to wish away later. The next step in rebuilding shattered communication bridges is to understand who's hurt and what actually happened. Calmly talking through the details squeezes out the heat of the moment and leaves room for logical discussion, admission of mistakes, and ultimately, forgiveness and reconciliation.

Your children can choose to forgive even when offended by someone who refuses to admit any wrong. Your child must do his part for peace but need never feel guilty if restoration falters. Conflict can be solved only by two-way communication. But your kids do have control over their parts of the problem.

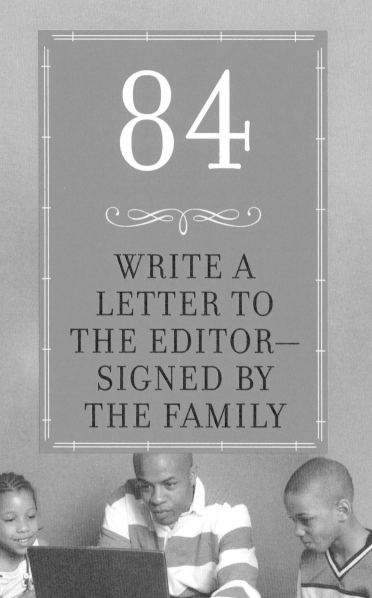

84

WRITE A
LETTER TO
THE EDITOR—
SIGNED BY
THE FAMILY

B are your soul. Come up with a hot-button issue that you and your children care about. Then put your passion into words in a convincing letter to the editor.

When writing such a letter, pick a specific topic. Clear focus makes every word count. Don't ever settle for sending the first draft. Keep at it until you've said exactly what you meant to say. Your message should be short and, if not sweet, at least respectful.

Many communiqués are ignored because the writer went for the jugular rather than approaching a delicate subject with finesse. There's a right way and a rude way to handle things. All too often logical thoughts get muddled because the letter writer's tone cuts cruelly instead of coming across as convincing.

The challenge in today's I-can-scream-louder-than-you-can society is to break through the harshness and get to the listening side, the place of peace. Your children should never be afraid to stand up for their convictions. But they must realize that their tone and approach tell others as much about them as the words chosen. Fill your letter with fussing and fuming and you'll come across as an irritating, clanging gong—not the voice of reason. Don't waste the time and energy.

Show them ways to win others over to their side with humor and kindheartedness. No one likes to feel forced into a choice. Conviction often creeps in quietly. Remember, you and your kids won't solve all the world's problems in a letter to the editor. But it's a way to speak out, to make their voices heard, to take responsibility for their citizenship, to get involved—and that's a powerful tool to give them before they launch out on their own.

85

PLAN A FAMILY TALENT SHOW—AND INVITE THE NEIGHBORS

G o ahead; toot that horn. Or play the piano. Or dance. You and your kids can come up with the best of the best of your many talents. Plan a program of no more than twenty minutes and start practicing. Elect a host to announce the acts and you're almost there. Now you just need an audience. Neighbors work, especially if you promise them food afterwards.

A family talent show flows smoother with a program listing every act. Give everyone a stage name if you'd like. Encourage even the youngest to work up a little something. You'll also need to decide where you'll perform. If you can't afford an auditorium, use a clean garage or any open room. Depending on the weather, your patio might work well. Before your guests arrive, set up seating. No matter what their spiritual perspective, make them feel God's welcome in your home.

Start the show with favorite sing-alongs like "Take Me Out to the Ball Game" or maybe "YMCA" for the younger set—anything that will loosen people up and allow them to relax. Even in the midst of missed notes, forgotten lines, or butterflies in the belly, the show must go on. Especially if you are the show.

Lead the way in applauding for each hardworking performer. From the most elaborate to the simplest act, every person with the gumption to go onstage deserves accolades for the effort. After the show, treat the whole audience and crew to a behind-the-scenes cast party. Put out simple treats, some sweet and some savory, and mingle with your guests. An ice sculpture, while quite classy, is completely optional.

86

GET CREATIVE IN THE KITCHEN

R ecipes were meant to be broken. Are you old-school in the kitchen? Do you carefully read every ingredient and never vary amounts? Maybe you're an "anything goes" kind of cook who makes scrumptious meals from leftovers. Either way, you can get more creative in the kitchen and pass along your flair for adventurous cooking to your kids.

Why turn up the spices or alter recipes? Because that's how you'll happen on improvements to old favorites. If you insist on making the same meals the same way every night, you'll find yourself with a mutiny on your hands. God loves variety: look at all the different people He made. Take that as your cue to explore new flavors, to taste adventure.

Remember that culinary changes rarely come naturally. We push back against modifying our favorite bread, for example. If it was good enough for Grandma, it's good enough for you. Maybe. But wouldn't it be tastier if you added sesame seeds, almond slivers, and a dollop of brown sugar before baking? Could be delicious.

You and your kids will never find out new ways to serve the family classics unless you experiment. Wild combinations sometimes work. And sometimes the results will be frighteningly foul. Keep a log of what's good and what's bad so you can improve on perfection and avoid making the same pungent mistake twice.

The other reason to help your kids feel comfortable on their own behind the stove is purely selfish. Someday you may want to retire from cooking. As your kids get older, it'd be nice if they could cook kickin' chili and cornbread or some other specialty. You'd get a break from the routine and they'd get a chance to shine in the kitchen. Once they're ready, step back to watch culinary magic (and maybe a little smoke) appear.

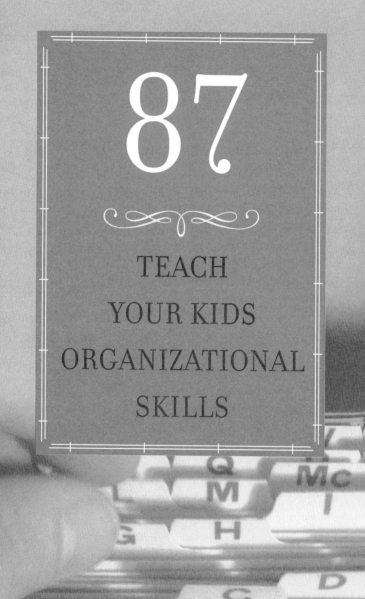

87

TEACH
YOUR KIDS
ORGANIZATIONAL
SKILLS

Clutter cramps your style. Your kids have probably felt the pinch too. Instead of jumping into their homework, how often do they waste time finding their mechanical pencil and scratch paper? Rather than getting down to the business at hand, they get stuck at the starting line.

Find a work space they can count on. Make sure they have the necessary tools close at hand. Nothing fancy, just some room to spread out, a place that will always be open and ready when they need it. Be sure they have proper lighting and comfortable chairs as well.

Even an organized person can become buried in paperwork. You get reading material in the mail, print off Web pages, and people send you more. Soon, you have too much to read. It's called "information overload." Divert the flood by focusing on the projects most important to you and your children. Help your kids decide what paperwork is worth exploring and what needs to be trashed.

Help your kids come up with their top ten goals. For example, if your kids want straight As, they'll need to study faithfully. That means setting aside certain hours for homework and cutting down on goof-off time. Let goals set their schedule and your kids can accomplish anything. Be sure you include important spiritual objectives, like Bible reading and prayer, in your to-do list as well.

Your children have more choices than you did at their age. Being organized means making the most of many opportunities and avoiding diversions that morph into procrastination. Hone down the best options from the good so they can succeed at what's most important to them.

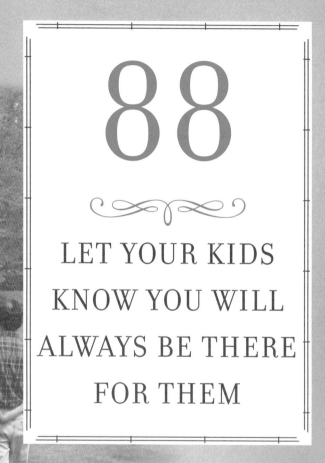

88

LET YOUR KIDS
KNOW YOU WILL
ALWAYS BE THERE
FOR THEM

Empty nests aren't all they're cracked up to be. Whether you're ready or not, the children will be gone and you and your spouse will anxiously await your kids' flights home. That's the way of the world and how growth occurs. Our young ones must mature and learn to fend for themselves, and their own children, as they create homes we long to visit. Part of your responsibility as a parent is preparing them for this inevitability.

This doesn't mean your kids won't be your kids forever. They will be. That's part of God's plan. You'll worry over them, pray over them, and thrill to their latest news. For years to come, you'll bask in their every accomplishment. Finally, roles may switch as with age you need greater care from them.

Your children should understand that you will always be available to them. That doesn't mean you'll provide twenty-four-hour loans or even pull them out of every jam. But you will assist them when helping is in their best interest. That's key: knowing when to pitch in and when to step aside. That's where prayer comes in. God can help you walk that delicate, fine line between helping and hindering.

Parenting is a balancing act. You feel your way, guess the rest, and that's OK. Praying for your kids regularly will benefit both you and them. Try handing over the reins to your kids for a time or certain purpose, then pulling them back. Let them go farther alone with each outing.

Remain willing to offer hope, help, and hindsight, assuming your kids will sit still long enough to listen. Being there for them means being ready to share your love and experience. It also means understanding that your offers of assistance may sometimes go unaccepted.

89

FLY HIGH WITH A KITE

K ites fuel flights of fancy, but they also require some practice. Sometimes it's a challenge. You need a combination
of puffy wind, solid craftsmanship, and an up-up-and-
away attitude. Releasing that soaring shadow gives you and your
kids the sensation of being in the air as well: darting and diving,
mischievous as the kite.

To make one from scratch, look online or in the library for help. You'll
be amazed at the possibilities. Or purchase a sturdy one at a toy
store. Either way, make the kite-building part of the adventure.
Allow enough time and be sure you have a secluded locale for the
construction. This is one time when you definitely don't want too
much wind.

Next comes launch and liftoff. Your experience may be similar to
that of many other would-be highflyers: multiple crash landings,
then success, then more spectacular dives. Just as you think you've
gotten that kite airborne, gravity grabs hold and yanks earthward.

Logical explanations fail you. The kite seems bent on going where
it will. Talk about how God's ways are kind of like that kite. We can
watch Him working and think we have everything figured out and
then, bam! He switches course and we begin to lose altitude.

Behind-the-scene forces are invisible to us, but not to God. We
may never understand, but He already does. Translation: the world
isn't a random, scary place. Meaning and order abound because
God's in control.

When a kite crashes, we try again. We extend the tail, pull harder
on the string, or pick a less-windy day. Whatever it takes. That's how
we should live our lives. God put hope within, along with the desire
to grow. Assist your kids in getting that stubborn kite into the air,
then step back and watch it soar.

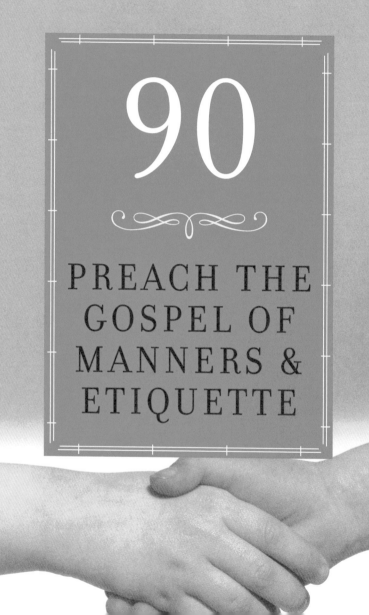

90

PREACH THE
GOSPEL OF
MANNERS &
ETIQUETTE

Good manners open doors. Literally. Your children will stand out like bright lights if they practice common courtesies. Listening without interrupting, letting another go first, and addressing elders with respect: these small sacrifices often mean the difference between getting a job and coming in second, between making a new friend or being ignored.

There are many lists of do's and don'ts when it comes to etiquette. People have created careers out of telling the rest of society what passes for polite. Make God's Golden Rule your measuring stick: do unto others as you would have them do unto you. Your children understand that inherently. They feel terrible when left out or insulted. When they are honored and included, the opposite is true. Their glowing smiles say it all.

Parents can be the biggest stumbling block to politeness. Yes, you. Letting your child get by with shoddy manners gives the green light for more of the same. There's nothing cute about Junior ignoring an elder when she talks to him. Allowing your daughter to treat another child with disdain will cause greater trouble down the line. Why? They learn that rudeness rules the day, unless you show and tell them otherwise.

Here are a few basics: Require your child's full attention when you're talking. Never allow him or her to talk back, or worse, strike you. If you do, you'll unleash a little monster who will grow more troublesome and tyrannical by the hour.

Show your children good manners in action. Examples work, and good examples work best. Politeness may be a dying art, but so what? You can take steps to cultivate its revival in your family. Live out the Golden Rule and put others first—simple but ever effective.

91

TRACE YOUR
CHILD'S
SILHOUETTE

Revive silhouette night. This country's forefathers and fore-mothers found great entertainment in setting up a bald light, seating the subject before it, and projecting a silhouette onto a grid on the wall. That same grid, in smaller scale, was printed on the paper before the artist. Capturing a likeness works well when you have the picture mapped out for you. Another approach involves tracing your child's silhouette on a piece of paper taped to the wall.

This intriguing exercise teaches patience, among other things. Your young models, for example, must sit still for some time. Minutes seem like hours. Doubtless your children will be anxious to see the pictures you've created. They'll want to know if they look beautiful or handsome. What do you think? That question burns bright in their eyes.

You have a God-ordained opportunity to tell your child the truth. In loving and direct words, explain how precious they are in God's sight—and yours. Your kids are stunning. See that God-glimmer within. As you trace their portraits, compliment their most lovely features, like long lashes, thick hair, and a strong chin.

Silhouettes hide the details and overlook imperfections. When you compliment your young subject, do the same. No reason to mention the latest crop of pimples or glasses that keep slipping. Build up your child with praise and make him or her feel good about God's creative genius.

As you look at the smooth edge of the silhouette, think about the edges of the souls within your care. Check for frays or tatters. The speed of life can choke out innocence before the roots have time to sink down. Protect the tender, exposed parts of their spirits and give your kids room to grow.

92

SAVE THE ENVIRONMENT

Who's in charge here? God, of course. Although He could miraculously solve every problem, God seeks your assistance. You and your kids should pitch in to keep this planet clean and well tended. Few disagree that the resources are limited.

When it comes to the health of the planet on which you live, you and your children can make an enormous difference. Decisions to be less wasteful translate into savings of water, food, and utilities. Not only does this put money back into your pocket, but your children learn to get by with less: no need to take a fifteen-minute soaking if a five-minute shower will do.

Teach your children conservation for God's sake: gratefully watching over this beautiful place, keeping its glow as perfect and pristine as possible. Don't you want your own family and those yet unborn to have the chance to see the splendor? The magnificence of an eight hundred-year-old redwood, big enough to park a car inside its trunk. A mountain stream so clear you can dip into the water and drink from your hands. A deep, lingering breath of clean, fresh air.

To bolster this concern for creation, pick a pet project as a family. Donate time, money, and enthusiasm to keeping your favorite location clean. You might even consider adopting a portion of a local highway so that everyone can see you care.

You and your children can take small steps to make great cumulative changes. Pass along healthy perspectives about the environment so they become family traditions. This unique world was specially prepared for us. Help your kids learn to respect the enormity of God's gift.

93

❧

MODEL THE
VALUE OF HARD
WORK & SELF-
DISCIPLINE

E ver since Adam and Eve got booted from paradise, humans have had to work—some harder than others, but we all have our tasks to bear. Different scenarios are but wishful thinking. Putting in the mandatory effort gets food on the table, a house overhead, and clothed kids. You have no choice except to make the best of things and neither do your children. What a great opportunity to show them what can be accomplished when they put their minds, hearts, and shoulders into the toil.

Teach your children to stay on task, and they'll be able to land enough work to keep them busy indefinitely. Bosses go batty trying to get staff members simply to do their jobs. Faithful employees, by contrast, are treasures. Teach your children to see tasks undone and pitch in to help. The world changes through self-starters who get in and fix what's broken.

Let your kids labor young. Have them husk corn, gather trash, set the table, make their beds, and dress themselves and younger siblings. You will have no problem coming up with possibilities. But the longer you wait to start training them right, the less responsive they'll be. You decide: small steps now or a giant uphill battle later.

Teach your kids that noble efforts arise out of a desire to please God—first and foremost. No other motivation matters. Scripture will tell you that's true. You'll never be satisfied waiting for appreciation from employers or other nine-to-fivers. But when you work out of a desire to serve God, your objectives change. Teach your children to work with vigor, make the most of opportunities, and rejoice that God watches over their labors with satisfaction.

94

HAVE A PAPER-AIRPLANE FLYING CONTEST

Contests spark competition. See this principle in action by sponsoring a build-your-own, fly-your-own paper airplane contest. This activity is both inexpensive and entertaining. See if any neighbor kids want in on the excitement. Start by finding the best basic flyer pattern you can and help your children create a flying machine from some old paper. Plane builders are limited only by their imaginations and materials on hand.

To ensure longer flights and easier plane recovery, go to an open field or school yard. That way you'll spend more time soaring and less roaming rooftops. Take turns so everyone can enjoy the spotlight for a moment.

Someone's plane may crumble in the contest. Though not exactly crashing and burning, one model or another often fails to make the grade and turns into a tumbling projectile. When this happens, help your young engineer see a couple of things.

Life is as fragile as that paper airplane. We must count on God's protective hand to get from one day to the next. And second, the contest's point is pure folly and fun. Reputation and honor don't hang in the balance, merely seeing whose plane flies the best and longest on one particular day. Remind all comers that there will be other days, other opportunities to take to the skies.

To help your kids remember the day with delight, no matter what happens, invest in some inexpensive ribbons for those who place and those who participate. Have a brief ceremony and give everyone a prize as well as plenty of verbal kudos. Your family will have a soft spot for their day at the races—the airplane races.

95

MOLD
FOOTPRINTS &
HANDPRINTS

igfoot lives. You'll believe it's true as your children continually pop the seams out of their shoes. Someday they'll tower over you. Now's the time to make memories so one day soon you can reflect together on how tiny they once were. Buy molding clay and have your young children make an imprint of a moment in time.

Even if your children are older, include them. You might need to buy a bigger frame, but that's okay. Give all your kids the same message. You treasure every stage of their growth. Incremental development switches into high gear as you and your children get more involved in the day-to-day drama of life. That's why freezing a moment in time now will be so meaningful later.

There are many ways to measure maturity. Talk to your kids about their growing hands, feet, and limbs. Bodies are getting bigger and stronger. What counts most, though, is their spiritual growth. Do they realize that God loves them wholly and completely? You can take steps to nurture their souls even as they're growing out of their clothes. Read the Bible to them, pray with them, and live your life as if you believe God is real.

Pick a special wall, maybe in your bedroom, where you'll line up these beautiful prints, these trophies of childhood. Years from now when that once tiny-footed toddler comes stomping into your house with a carload of grandchildren, the whole crew will gather in amazement. That was Dad's foot? Mom's handprint? They won't believe it's possible until you tell them about the day you took the time to create a treasure.

96

CREATE &
BURY A TIME
CAPSULE

Our present was their future. Those who have gone before us dreamed of this very day. Wished they could be here. They tried to imagine what types of homes you'd have, cars you'd drive, food you'd eat. You and your children are doing things that people a generation ago wouldn't believe.

That's the beauty of the time capsule. You have the chance to create a storehouse of memorabilia that will intrigue someone else someday. For starters, take the front page of a newspaper to provide a slice of time. Maybe take off labels from foods or gadgets—anything that represents who you are and what you did. Write a list of your favorite movies and books.

Create a letter that describes everyone in your family. Include a stack of photos. Tuck in a small gospel tract that tells discoverers how they can get to know God. Jot a note explaining why He's so important in your life. Then bury everything in a waterproof, rust-proof container at least several feet underground.

Creating a time capsule gives a gift to the future. You probably will miss the grand reopening, but this isn't about you. That's one of the main points to share with your kids. You're passing along a snapshot that some future family could never experience. You'll never know how much they appreciate that you cared enough to share your lives.

Life goes on. Someday it will continue without you and your chance for impact will pass. Make your mark on your child's heart while it's malleable. You have no idea how many more opportunities you'll have or what the future holds. But you can invest now so that when they open their time capsule of memory, they'll pull out many mementos of joy.

97

PITCH A
TENT—
INDOORS

A dventure doesn't have to be your middle name. Even if you're a timid mom or dad, you can give your kids a taste of the wild outdoors in your own living room. Create a woodsy setting by pitching a tent or two. No need to pound the stakes into your carpet; just pile up a few heavy books to hold them in place.

Pull out some old sleeping bags, grab pillows off the beds, and prepare for a night of fun. Find a tape with wild sounds on it. That way you can enjoy the noise of nature without worrying about bug spray.

Have your kids gather up their largest stuffed animals to create a perimeter of intrigue. Instead of s'mores around a campfire, melt a marshmallow in the microwave and layer it on a chocolate bar between two graham crackers. No one better complain that the marshmallowy center isn't burnt to a crisp!

Before bed, tell stories of brave women and men who molded our country. Talk of travelers who covered ground in covered wagons. Tell some Paul Bunyan tall tales or pick other stories from your shelf. Safely light a few candles and enjoy the quiet glow. Sing some camp songs if you'd like before hitting the sack.

The only thing you'll miss (besides rummaging skunks) are the stars overhead. Remedy this by telling your kids about how God sees them no matter where they are, even in a tent, in a cave, or under the ebony of night. Your kids have His full attention. He loves them in all places and at all times. What a wonderful message to reflect upon before slumber.

98

ORGANIZE A
SEARCH FOR
TEDDY BEARS
IN THE DARK

Not lions, not tigers, but bears, oh my! One of the greatest delights of childhood is being surprised. Bring your kids a bundle of joy by organizing a full-blown, deep-in-the-heart-of-the-forest bear hunt. In your own home.

First, gather every stuffed bear in the house. If you can't come up with at least a dozen, go door-to-door borrowing from neighbors. Most homes host many more. One of you will occupy the children while the other runs through the house looking for adequate but not too terribly complicated hiding places. Stow the bears so your youngest children will be able to find them. If you have a mix of children, let the oldest do the hiding. They'll love it!

What comes next is pure excitement. Hand that child a flashlight and head to the hunting grounds. Turn out all other lights and keep close by. Let that one beam of light lead the way. And then follow your bear hunters around as they look for the sneaky beasts. As you find each bear, the thrill builds. Your children will want to rush from one bear burrow to the next. Let them, guiding enough to keep them from walking into furniture or walls. Then applaud their efforts with each new find!

Once your little hunter has caught the quota, flip on the lights. They'll probably want another round as soon as possible. And you'll have a brand-new family tradition. Tell them that sometimes they have only a dim light to lead the way, only a glimmer of hope. But they should know that God, like any good parent, stands waiting in the darkness, protecting and guiding them, and He's always there if they call.

99

MAKE A SWING FOR EVEN THE OLDEST KIDS

I f only swings were immortal. Maybe yours is on its last leg. Sooner or later it'll start falling apart. They always do. Chances are that a houseful of kids and their friends put it to the test. That's the way life works. Nothing, not even the good things man makes, lasts forever. That means we'll have to wait a while to see what kind of swings God created for His heavenly mansions.

A worn-out swing set, however, usually means that the young users have started to grow up. Your children are no longer little kids but are closing in on the tween, teen, or even college years. They could be heading out the door soon.

Doesn't matter—they still like to rock. Maybe it's a long-forgotten memory of the cradle, but kids of every age love the feeling. That's why rocking chairs and porch swings never go out of style. And that's why you should be sure that you maintain a sturdy swing for your older children to enjoy. Doubtless the younger set will spend many happy hours there as well, listening to stories or merely enjoying the day.

Children, even the most mature, like a place to get lost in their thoughts. They long for time and space to dream. That's what you provide when you build a big, strong swing and tell them it's earmarked just for the older kids. They may look at you funny at first, but don't be surprised when it becomes their favorite piece of furniture.

A swing for big kids—it's an idea whose time has come. And maybe, if you ask nicely, they'll let you use it too.

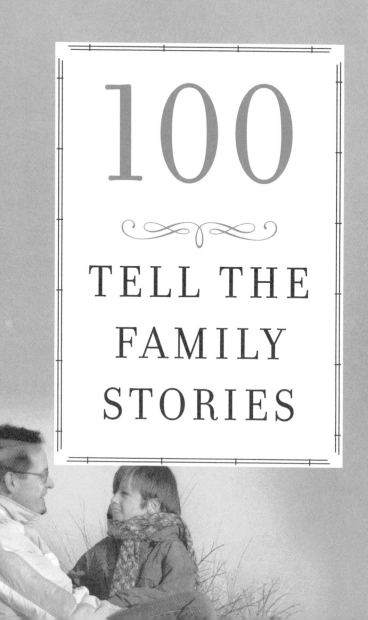

100

TELL THE
FAMILY
STORIES

So many stories, so little time. You hold within your mind an enormous storehouse of gold. Only you can tell your kids what they looked like as babies, about their first words, and how cute they were when they sat primly on their potty-chairs. The tales don't end there. As your family grows, you'll have the opportunity to discover even more about your beloved little (and big) ones. Don't keep those stories to yourself.

Instead, jot them down or take the time to plant a precious scene in their minds. Lock the fun into memory banks so that they can retell them when they're old enough to appreciate the silliness, sadness, fun, and drama. As your kids mature, be brave enough to give them the scoop on what you were like as a kid. Maybe they'll learn from your mistakes—just as you did.

Tell your children how you and your spouse met. Drag your kids along as you meander down memory lane. They actually enjoy hearing a humorous anecdote from their parents' past. Your struggles and triumphs make you more real, more accessible. Your honesty gives them food for thought. Most of all, you give them a repertoire of delightful family stories for their children and their children's children. And so legends grow.

Storytelling is how we learn. Parables teach where sermons fail. Make every day an opportunity to show and tell your children eternal truths. Choose your words wisely. Pour into them the excitement of being a part of a grand plan. And let them hear the greatest story of all, about a beloved Son who gives eternal life to all who believe in Him. Your kids belong in God's big picture, His sweeping story.

101

PUT A
PREMIUM
ON PEACE

You may have learned about relationship with God in the home you grew up in, discovered it on your own later—or you may even now be seeking the peace that comes only from knowing God and His love. Perhaps it's something you long to give your children before they leave your nest and take up residence in a big, chaotic world. The good news of the gospel is that God has made peace available to anyone who asks—that means you.

When Jesus was born in a small Middle-Eastern town called Bethlehem more than two thousand years ago, the angels announced to shepherds watching their flocks in nearby fields that the Prince of Peace had arrived. "Go and find Him," they told the shepherds. "This is what generations before you have been waiting for!" So important was the message that the angels bypassed kings and delivered it to everyday people who were busy doing their everyday jobs.

Jesus Christ, of whom the angels spoke, had been sent to make peace between God and man. He accomplished His mission by living a perfect life and dying a perfect death—a death in which He paid the price for every sinful thought you have ever had, every hurtful word you have ever uttered, every ungodly action, every mistake, every single thing that mars the purity and beauty with which God created you. Then He rose again to finish the transaction—His gift to you and for you, peace with God the Father, both now and for eternity.

Put a premium on peace in your life and your home. Model it before your children and be quick to tell them its Source. It's the greatest gift you can give yourself and your kids—before they leave home.

THOUGHTS OF JOY FOR LIFE'S JOURNEY

He who helps a child helps humanity with an immediateness
which no other help given to human creatures in any other stage of
human life can possibly give again.

Phillips Brooks

The best compliment to a child or a friend is the feeling you give him that
he has been set free to make his own inquiries, to come to conclusions
that are right for him, whether or not they coincide with your own.

Alistair Cooke

The soul is healed by being with children.

Fyodor Dostoevsky

BEFORE MY KIDS LEAVE
HOME, I'D LIKE TO . . .

THOUGHTS OF JOY FOR LIFE'S JOURNEY

We tend to glorify adulthood and wisdom and worldly prudence, but the gospel reverses all this. The gospel says that the inescapable condition of entrance into the divine fellowship is that we turn and become as a little child. As against our natural judgment we must become tender and full of wonder and unspoiled by the hard skepticism on which we so often pride ourselves. But when we really look into the heart of a child, willful as he may be, we are often ashamed. God has sent children into the world, not only to replenish it, but to serve as sacred reminders of something ineffably precious which we are always in danger of losing. The sacrament of childhood is thus a continuing revelation.

ELTON TRUEBLOOD

All thy children shall be taught of the Lord;
and great shall be the peace of thy children.

ISAIAH 54:13 KJV

BEFORE MY KIDS LEAVE HOME, I'D LIKE TO . . .

THOUGHTS OF JOY FOR
LIFE'S JOURNEY

*We find a delight in the beauty and happiness of children
that mades the heart too big for the body.*

AUTHOR UNKNOWN

*While we try to teach our children all about l ife,
our children teach us what life is all about.*

ANGELA SCHWINDT

*You can learn many things from children.
How much patience you have, for instance.*

FRANKLIN P. JONES

BEFORE MY KIDS LEAVE HOME, I'D LIKE TO . . .

THOUGHTS OF JOY FOR LIFE'S JOURNEY

Before I got married, I had six theories
about bringing up children;
now I have six children and no theories.

JOHN WILMOT
EARL OF ROCHESTER

Raising children is a creative endeavor,
an art, rather than a science.

BRUNO BETTELHEIM

We begin by imagining that we are giving to [children];
we end by realizing that they have enriched us.

POPE JOHN PAUL II

BEFORE MY KIDS LEAVE HOME, I'D LIKE TO . . .

THOUGHTS OF JOY FOR LIFE'S JOURNEY

The potential possibilities of any child
are the most intriguing and stimulating in all creation

RAY L. WILBUR

Don't you see that children are God's best gift?
the fruit of the womb his generous legacy?
Like a warrior's fistful of arrows
are the children of a vigorous youth.
Oh, how blessed are you parents,
with your quivers full of children!

PSALM 127:3-5 MSG

Point your kids in the right direction—
when they're old they won't be lost.

PROVERBS 22:6 MSG

BEFORE MY KIDS LEAVE HOME, I'D LIKE TO . . .